A Somerset Airman

The story of an RAF Armourer, 1939–1946.

Eric Gardner

ISIS

LARGE PRINT

Oxford

First published in Great Britain 2005
by Red'N'Ritten Ltd.

Published in Large Print 2006 by ISIS Publishing Ltd.,
7 Centremead, Osney Mead, Oxford OX2 0ES
by arrangement with
Red'N'Ritten Ltd.

British Library Cataloguing in Publication Data
Gardner, Eric
    A Somerset airman. – Large print ed. –
(Isis reminiscence series)
1. Gardner, Eric
2. World War, 1939–1945 – Personal narratives,
British 3. Large type books
I. Title
940.5'44941'092

ISBN 0–7531–9352–3 (hb)
ISBN 978–0–7531–9353–2 (pb)

Printed and bound in Great Britain by
T. J. International Ltd., Padstow, Cornwall

IN MEMORIAM

This book is dedicated
to the memory of
Eric Bertram Gardner,
a much-loved husband,
father and grandfather.

Eric Bertram Gardner 1921–2004

Contents

Preface

The story of an RAF Armourer 1939–1946.
by Eric Gardner

Eric Gardner grew up in Frome on a small family farm. The *Introduction* to this book is his account of the farm itself, daily routines and the animals with which he shared his childhood, and paints an engaging picture of rural life in 1930s Somerset.

At the age of 19 he joined the RAF. His witty observations of day-to-day life as an Airman in wartime Britain and Canada give a fascinating insight into the life experienced by many ordinary men and women, from all backgrounds, who were brought together by World War Two.

Like many of his generation, Eric Gardner did not receive a higher education, and was unable to fulfil his obvious potential. In later life he often commented that the RAF had been his university.

Eric thought his wartime experiences would be of little interest to anyone else, because he did not see any active service. His family did not agree and encouraged him to commit his memories to paper.

He finished the manuscript for *A Somerset Airman* just days before his sudden death at the age of 82 and so, sadly, Eric never saw it in print.

Preface by Jean Gardner and Katherine Moon
(Author's daughters)

Introduction

Flint House Farm, Frome, Somerset 1930s–1950s

Flint House

Flint House was probably built in the early or mid nineteenth century, but little is known of its history prior to its occupation by my grandparents, Ann and Albert Cullen, during the first decade of the twentieth century. A perusal of the Census Returns from 1841 onwards is needed to identify the nineteenth century occupants and might give an indication of its age.

It was a stone built, four-bedroom house with outbuildings and two acres of land, which suggests that the original owner must have been comfortably off. On the Ordnance Survey, large-scale map (25 inches to a mile) of 1889 it is described as Flint's House, but it was known by my family as Flint House.

Flints Farm was a few hundred yards away and a little further on a row of cottages called Flints Cottages. How the name was arrived at I have no idea, because no flints were used in its construction nor, as far as I

1

know, were any found in the vicinity. Maybe a family name is involved.

My grandparents obtained it a few years before the start of the First World War and lived there until my grandmother's death in 1933. My father, Bertie Gardner then bought it and lived there with his family until his death in 1939. Afterwards, his widow continued to stay there with her elder son, Clifford, from where he carried on the business, and continued to live with his wife when they married in 1947.

Eventually, Cliff sold it to the local council in the early 1970s, for building. The house was demolished and a housing estate built on the site and the surrounding fields. No trace at all remains of the house or its land. Situated on the South Western edge of Frome, Flint House was about three quarters of a mile from the town centre and a half mile from the nearest shop and public house. It was reached by a lane that led off the nearest road, Green Lane, formerly Marston Back Lane. The lane was called Puddingbag Lane: believed to indicate that it was a cul-de-sac; this it certainly was, because after proceeding for about a quarter of a mile it ended in a field.

For the first thirty or forty yards it provided access to a row of four or five terraced cottages: Albion Place. Two hundred yards further on it passed the entrance to the hundred-yard drive up to Flint House. The lane continued for another two hundred yards before terminating at the gateway to a large field. It was much used by cattle from a neighbouring farm, driven backwards and forwards, to and from the various fields

2

abutting the lane. Consequently, in wet weather it was very muddy.

It was completely unlit; the nearest streetlight was on the roadside near Albion Cottages. Anyone visiting on foot at night needed a good torch if they were to avoid the large puddles and patches of mud. It was not a walk to be undertaken wearing dainty footwear. Those leaving Flint House quite often wore Wellingtons as far as the end of the lane, then put on shoes, leaving their boots under the hedge ready for the return journey.

As mentioned earlier the house was reached via a hundred yard drive leading off Puddingbag Lane. The drive had a five-barred gate at its entrance to keep the livestock in and was fenced on the south side bordering the orchard and garden for the same reason. The side bordering the paddock, however, was not fenced, so livestock could wander onto the drive if they wished, which was not welcomed by all visitors.

The drive was well drained and normally quite dry, which was a relief after the mud of Puddingbag Lane. However, it was completely unlit so a torch was needed at night to avoid walking into any animal that might be there, and also to dodge any deposits of manure. At the end of the drive was a little gate giving access to the path to the front and back doors.

There was a small porch at the front door with wooden shelves normally used to display pot plants. The front door led into a small hall with stairs leading off it, and doors to the sitting room on the left and living room on the right. In the 1930s the sitting room was normally used only for special occasions, but later on, during the 1939–45 war, it was used as a living room by evacuees, and subsequently by my mother when she shared the house with her son and his wife. It was rather damp, as the house had no damp course, and moisture often rose two or three feet above the skirting board to the great detriment of the wallpaper.

The living room was smaller and cosier, but also suffered from the lack of a damp course and wet patches were much in evidence. It had a large, straight chimney and occasionally a sooty bird would emerge from it and cause havoc in its attempt to escape through a closed window. In my grandmother's time, on a shelf was a stuffed red squirrel in a glass case, which as a small boy I greatly coveted. On her death it disappeared during the clearance of her effects.

The house had neither gas nor electricity, which was not installed until the 1950s, and lighting was provided by an ornate paraffin lamp hanging from the ceiling; taller members of the family had to be careful. The piano, much used at all the parties, had a candle fitting at each side, which were used to supplement the light from the lamp. At one party a guest turned round with his back to the piano, the better to give a rendering of a popular ballad, and the candle set fire to the back of his jacket. It was quickly extinguished by a hastily thrown glass of beer.

There were many such lively parties at the farm, and they all followed a similar pattern. Soon after arriving the men would adjourn to the local pub, leaving the women to have a gossip at home and prepare the supper. Ladies did not generally go into public houses, and on the few occasions they did, they went to a "best room" well away from the public bar.

At ten o'clock or even later, the men would return with drinks for the women and more beer for themselves. And then someone would sit down at the piano, and the party would start; general singing and some dancing, a waltz or two and even a quickstep, would be performed on the limited floor space available. Sometimes my father could be persuaded to give a rendering of his favourite song "Oh, Oh Antonio" and everyone would join in the chorus.

One of my uncles had a little dog that he claimed to have taught to sing the National Anthem. Sure enough, when he struck up the opening chords, and at a given signal, the dog would sit up and yowl away. This would incite our dog into a fit of barking, which rather spoiled the performance.

During the party there would be a break for supper, which generally included cold ham, pigs' feet, chitterlings, pickled eggs, pickled walnuts and Gorgonzola cheese. Highly indigestible if taken late at night, but apparently consumed without ill effect. On one occasion when relatives arrived unexpectedly, or perhaps in greater numbers than anticipated, I was sent down to the local fish and chip shop (Birtwistle's) to buy twenty portions of fish and chips. I was about nine or ten and felt quite proud to be entrusted with this mission, and also enjoyed the expression of surprise in the queue behind me at such a large order.

These parties would often continue until the small hours, even though my father had to be up at six o'clock the next morning to milk the cows and deliver the milk to his customers.

From the late thirties our wireless, a Cossor, I believe, took the place on the shelf previously occupied by my late grandmother's red squirrel. The wireless was powered by a dry battery and an accumulator, which had to be taken to the local electrical shop each week to be re-charged at the cost of sixpence a time. So, two accumulators were needed, one in use and one at the shop. At £1, the dry battery was quite expensive.

There would be some consternation when it started to run down, and we tried to manage with reduced volume in an attempt to prolong its life a little longer. On one occasion, as a result of receiving some rather dubious advice, Father put it in the oven for a while in an attempt to rejuvenate it; it didn't help, it only made it sticky.

We listened to Variety on a Saturday night (Robb Wilton, Stainless Stephen, Gracie Fields, etc.), the occasional play and Henry Hall's Late Night Dance Music. In this room on the morning of 3rd September 1939 I heard the declaration of war against Germany and saw my mother weep, as she had two sons of military age.

A door from the living room led into the kitchen. This was rather narrow, with a kitchen range against one wall and a large dresser on the other. There was a table under the window on which we had breakfast and any other impromptu meals. Hard wearing coconut matting was on the floor. Sometimes, from a hook set into the ceiling, a piece of home cured bacon was suspended, providing a landing ground for the occasional fly, probably fresh from a sojourn in the less savoury parts of the farmyard.

From the kitchen a door led into a small pantry; this was a flimsy, makeshift structure built on, not too expertly, to the back of the house. It had a concrete slab under the window on which foodstuffs could be stored. However, the window had several small panes missing, and ivy and other climbing plants outside would thrust tendrils through, as if seeking to help themselves to the items on the shelf. Periodically these had to be cut back, but they always returned. No attempt was made to repair the window.

Because of the defects in its structure the pantry was not mouse-proof and these marauders would occasionally find their way in. As the cat was not allowed in — a bowl of cream would be more tempting than any mouse — traps were set, baited with cheese. These were supposed to be checked daily, but generally weren't, which did little for the hygiene of the pantry. In those days there was a more relaxed attitude to such matters.

Another door from the kitchen led to a narrow passageway to the dairy. On leaving the kitchen, there was on the left the entrance to a dark cupboard under the stairs that housed old coats, unwanted items and large spiders. The passage walls were just rough stone that had been whitewashed — and this would come off on clothes if rubbed against. The floor, too, had uneven surfaces and there was a drain on one side, useful for the kitchen, but into which the unwary could step.

The dairy, which also had rough whitewashed walls and a stone floor, had many functions. In it was the only tap in the house from which all the water required in the household and also for the livestock was drawn. Unfortunately, there was a permanent problem with this tap: it only delivered a slow stream of water so a bucket was kept underneath to ensure a supply of water was always available.

There was a copper, underneath which a fire could be lit to provide hot water for baths, laundry . . . The zinc bath was also in the dairy and, as this room was unheated and both door and window let in copious draughts, bath night in the winter was not a cosy occasion.

Naturally, the room was also used as a dairy, in that buckets of milk would be kept there and milk bottles filled ready for delivery to customers. Churns, buckets and bottles would be cleansed with hot water and afterwards the floor would be mopped dry. A separator was used to produce cream. Milk was poured into a large bowl on its top and a handle turned many times to produce a thin stream of cream from one spout and skimmed milk from another. This took quite a long time and turning the handle was an unwelcome chore for me sometimes.

There was also a butter churn in the dairy, as butter was made from surplus cream. This was most likely to be done in warm weather when, in the absence of any type of refrigeration, surpluses had to be dealt with quickly. In an attempt to prevent milk going off the milk churns were stood in tubs of cold water, which was generally sufficient for overnight storage, but not much longer in very warm weather. Making butter could be a tedious business, especially in sultry weather when it seemed to take a long time to form. Much turning of the churn handle was required — another unwelcome chore. By-products of these activities were skimmed milk, buttermilk and, quite often, sour milk as well; all of which were fed to the pigs. The dairy was the main workplace of the house and was nearly always the scene of some activity.

The door from the dairy led out to the farmyard. Originally there was a pump just outside this door, but the only time I saw it used it was a disappointment. After much vigorous pumping it eventually coughed up just a small quantity of a strange-coloured liquid. When my father took over the house he removed it and filled in the well.

Upstairs there were four bedrooms, two at the front and two at the back. Only three were in use. Mother and Father had one, my brother and I shared another — not only the room, but also the bed. The third room, at the back of the house, was kept for visitors. In between times it was used for various purposes: storing potatoes and apples . . . Once Father bought a cheap incubator through mail order and put it in this room to hatch chickens. Unfortunately, he got the settings wrong; it overheated and cracked all the eggs, which was the end of the enterprise. Much later, in the 1950s, my brother converted this room into a bathroom.

Lighting upstairs was by candles only. Oil lamps were not used.

Finally there was the lavatory and its location outside could be a problem, particularly at night. It could only be reached by the path that went round the house, and as this was unlit, again, a torch was needed. A candle and matches were kept in the lavatory, but the door had such big gaps in it that draughts frequently blew out the candle. The only compensation was that the occupant could no longer see the very large spiders that lurked there. Originally there had been a flush toilet, but this had long ceased to operate. The cistern was still there, but it was no more than a rusted piece of metal. Probably it had frozen up one cold winter long ago and never been repaired. Things tended not to get repaired at Flint House.

The toilet drained into a cesspit located near the pigsty, some distance away and the method of flushing was to carry a bucket of water from the dairy and pour it down. There were two hazards in this. Firstly, it was difficult not to slop the water over your legs while carrying it round the house, and secondly, it was hard to avoid getting it over the seat when pouring it in, to the discomfort of the next occupant.

Further hazards awaited the unwary at night. A very large yucca plant in the front garden was much too close to the path and its needle-sharp leaves ruined many a lady's stockings if they strayed onto the path edge.

Finally, there were the cows from our neighbour's farm. At night they would often congregate by the low wall separating the path from the field, no doubt using the house as a shelter from the wind. Sometimes they would hang their heads over the wall. Visitors to the lavatory might well hear a loud "Moo" or other bovine noise coming out of the darkness, or get a glimpse of a cow's head. Nervous visitors found this unsettling and sometimes completely lost the will to continue the journey, and returned to the house with their story of a close encounter with a large beast.

The residents of Flint House, being well used to the sanitary arrangements, were perhaps less sympathetic with the qualms of some visitors than they should have been. A commode and chamber pot were kept upstairs for anyone too nervous to make the journey.

Outbuildings, Yards and Paddocks

When he took over Flint House, just outside the back door, my father erected a lean-to shed. This occupied some of the space previously used by the pump. It was used as a bike shed, workshop, storage for tools and garden implements, etc. It also housed an incubator, more efficient than the one that had been kept in the house. The eggs still had to be turned by hand twice a day — another tedious chore for a small boy. As there was no electricity any work in the shed at night had to be done by the uncertain and flickering light of a paraffin fuelled hurricane lantern.

Joined to the dairy and along one side of the farmyard were the stable and cowshed. These were substantial stone-built buildings. The stable rarely had a horse in it; our pony stayed outside in all weathers. It had to be extreme before he would come into the farmyard seeking shelter. The stable was divided into two parts by a wooden partition. One side was used for general storage and for odd jobs such as chopping firewood and sawing wood . . . In the other, poultry and cow food was stored in large bins, with no lids. If the door was left open the hens would help themselves.

Rats, too, sometimes found their way in. It was not very well lit and on one occasion my grandfather had an unpleasant experience; he reached into the bin to scoop out poultry food, and a rat ran up his arm to escape through the door. Thereafter, everyone was more circumspect when getting food for the hens.

Over the stable was a loft reached by a vertical ladder fastened to the wall. An exciting place for a boy to explore, but a little risky, because it was rather dark and there were some holes in the floor. Very little was stored there — except some hay and straw and a few old sacks. The farm cats sometimes chose to have their kittens there.

This loft was always called the tallet, a name I accepted without question. Many years later when reading a book about Wessex dialects I found a reference to it: "A hay loft over a stable or similar building."

Next to the stable was the cowshed, which was big enough to take three or four cows, but generally they only went in to be milked. The cows, like the pony, stayed outside in the field all the year round.

The cowshed was frequently used to house young calves being weaned; when taken away from their mothers, they had to be taught to drink warm milk from a bucket. This needed a little patience as the calves were accustomed to putting their heads up to suckle from their mother's udder and had to be taught to put their heads down to drink from the bucket. Whoever was doing the weaning would dip his finger in the milk and allow the calf to suck this whilst at the same time coaxing it to put its head down to drink from the bucket. This generally worked, but sometimes the calf would instinctively raise its head sharply and as even young calves are quite strong there would be a struggle to control it during which the bucket could get tipped over. Anyone struggling to feed a stubborn calf would get milk slopped over them, their toes trodden on and at worst slip over on a floor covered with spilt milk and cow dung.

However, it could be an entertaining spectacle for an onlooker; and I remember my grandfather chuckling whilst watching my brother struggling in this way, and calling out "Casn't 'old 'im then!"

At right angles to the cow stall and forming the second side of the farmyard were the pigsties. Between the two buildings was quite a large covered area, but open on the side facing the farmyard. In this would be stored various farming implements, such as hay rakes. There was also a large rusty item, like a great mincer, intended for cutting up mangel-wurzels for cattle feed. I believe this had not been used in living memory, it filled up a corner and just rusted away. Next to it was an old boiler used for boiling up potatoes (the small and discarded ones) to mix in with the pig food. This had one disadvantage in that it leaked slightly onto the fire beneath and would put it out unless stoked up energetically.

Also bales of straw, used as seating by the farm cats keeping an eye out for rats and mice on their way to pilfer food from the pigsties, would be stored in the covered area.

The two sties were simple affairs, just a covered area and open pens. Normally one was kept for a sow waiting to farrow and the other for the two or three pigs being fattened for market. Occasionally, there would be an escape through the none-too-secure door and responding to the alarm call, "The pigs are out!" everyone would turn out to help return them to their sties. This would generally be achieved by using the lure of a bucket of pig food.

Bordering the farmyard opposite the pigsties was the henhouse. This was comparatively new. It was purpose built, and had been delivered in sections and assembled in situ with some difficulty. There were one or two large gaps between roof and walls that should not have been there, but it served its purpose as a safe house for the poultry. Adjoining it was an old shed, open on one side and with an earth floor where the hens would congregate in wet weather. In here individual coops for broody hens sitting on eggs were kept; Father considered the natural way was best. These had to be carefully secured at night to guard against marauding foxes.

Just outside the back door, separated by a wooden fence from the path round the house was the farmyard, around which were grouped the farm buildings previously described. The farmyard itself had a rough and stony surface, as from time to time stone and rubble would be thrown down to fill in the puddles. It was big enough for cars and even visiting lorries to turn round in and the centre was kept clear for this purpose.

Stacked around the edge were odd pieces of timber and an accumulation of discarded or "one day to be mended" items such as cracked pig troughs, hen coops without doors, handle-less shovels . . . Hens patrolled it on the lookout for scraps that might be thrown out from the house. Cows from the field were free to wander in and frequently did, and of course left their deposits, which was a nuisance if you wanted to cross it at night.

At the far end close to the perimeter hedge, far enough away from the house not to be offensive, but near the pigsties from which most of it was obtained, was a sizeable dung heap. Near it, in the corner made by the two perimeter hedges, but hidden underground, was the cesspit that served the house. I don't remember this ever being emptied and it probably overflowed into the ditch at the other side of the hedge, bordering our neighbour's field. This corner did indeed smell a little strong in hot weather, but with the dung heap and pigsties also in close proximity it was not surprising.

Somewhere in or near the farmyard was the farm wheelbarrow. This had been made by my maternal grandfather — Granfer Vowles — and given to Father as a gift. It had, however, severe limitations. My grandfather was a carpenter who worked in a local colliery and was used to repairing coal trucks and other equally robust pieces of equipment. He built the wheelbarrow to a similar sturdy standard using thick wood. It was large, had an iron wheel and even when empty was heavy to push, but as it was a gift from his father-in-law, Father had to make use of it. It was kept outside, perhaps in the over-optimistic hope that it might rot away, but its constant soaking with rain made it even heavier.

When moving manure, which was its main function, it could only be half-filled and even then Father would struggle to push it, especially in wet weather when its great iron wheel would sink into the ground. A visiting uncle lending a hand with farm work was heard to exclaim, "Thick girt barra be made for giants." It was quite indestructible and lingered around the farm even in later days when my brother bought a lighter wheelbarrow. It was always there ready to test the strength of anyone who ventured to use it.

In front of the house was a small lawn with an old garden seat in the corner, for when we had our tea outside. The lawn was just big enough to play clock golf

16

and a flowerpot was sunk into the ground for this purpose. On one side, with a few flowers that tended to suffer from the continual retrieval of the ball, there was a border, and in it, much too close to the path, was the notorious yucca plant with needle-sharp leaves ready to inflict a painful stab to anyone incautious enough to approach.

A gate from the lawn led to the vegetable garden, which was quite productive due, no doubt, to the liberal application of the contents of the dung heap. All vegetables used in the kitchen were grown there and none were bought from the shops.

The orchard was about three quarters of an acre, but had no more than half a dozen trees. Part was fenced off for poultry and one or two mobile poultry houses were located there. The remainder was used for extra grazing for the pony or calves. A popular tree was a Beauty of Bath, which produced small red apples in August, much earlier than other varieties. One bore large quantities of cooking apples. But everyone's favourite was an old tree, Tom Putt, that had large red fruit, the choicest of all apples.

Long after the farm was demolished and the orchard built upon I was in a church in Devon and saw a memorial plaque to Thomas Putt "A horticulturalist of distinction and developer of new strains of apples." During the intervening years I had never seen or heard of this apple, but the memory remained with me, until quite recently whilst visiting a National Trust house in North Wales we saw an exhibition of old species of apples, and prominent amongst them was a dish of Tom

Putts described as a late eighteenth century species. They were large red apples looking just as delicious as I remembered. Sadly, none were for sale.

The paddock was just over an acre. It sloped down from the drive to a drainage ditch in the centre. Part of the drainage was in underground pipes, but this had not been completed along the full length, so the remaining length was an open ditch. At one time there was a small pond in the corner of the paddock where frogs and newts could be found, but this was later filled in to the detriment of the drainage of the paddock, which could be very boggy in wet weather.

Drinking water for the livestock was provided in a large and rather ugly bath that presumably had been obtained from a demolished house. This had to be filled from the single tap in the dairy, a laborious job when several cows or calves had to be supplied with fresh water. The bath was also used to drown unwanted kittens produced by the farm cats.

The hedges were always a problem. They needed to be cut each year and also made stock proof to prevent calves breaking through into the neighbour's field. Gaps in the hedge were blocked with barbed wire and occasionally discarded bedsteads, which did not improve the appearance of the hedgerow, but served the purpose and had the advantage of being an instant remedy.

Farm animals

My grandfather kept no dogs at the farm, but when my father took over, and afterwards my brother, there was a succession of dogs. On moving in, we brought from our previous house a small black and white mongrel called Spot. She was already elderly, but settled down quite well. Unfortunately she had a predilection to roll in manure; and as this was readily available both in the farmyard and in the field, she always had to be bathed before being allowed into the house.

When she died she was replaced by a small spaniel named Pat, which we had from my father's brother. She was a quiet inoffensive little creature and made little impact on our lives.

Her replacement was a different kettle of fish entirely and warrants his tale to be told: Mick was a handsome black and white mongrel with a good deal of hound in him. He was about a year old when given to my brother, by someone in the town who said he thought he might be a good farm dog. He couldn't have been more wrong; Mick was boisterous and wild. At every opportunity, when released from his lead, he tore round and round the paddock at top speed, scattering the hens in all directions and chasing the calves.

He had large feet that always seemed to be muddy and a perpetually wagging tail. Mick was soon banned from the house, after chasing a cat and upsetting a table, and tearing the curtains. He found his way into the hen house and ate, with great relish, any eggs he found. Father tried to break him of this habit by filling

19

an empty eggshell with bread thickly smeared with mustard, but Mick ate that, too, and just cooled his mouth by drinking the calves' water.

It was then decided that he would have to be tied up and only let loose under strict supervision. My brother made a kennel and the dog was chained up in the farmyard, to the relief of the other animals. The cats could once again patrol the farmyard, keeping just out of Mick's reach — which would send him into a frenzy of frustrated barking. Even the calves learned that they could now safely look at their tormentor.

My brother then met a man in a pub who said he was looking for a young dog as company for his wife. Mick was promptly offered and arrangements were made to take him to his new home. This was done the following afternoon, but the wife was in bed suffering from a migraine so her husband said they would just have the dog for a few days' trial.

Everything was going well until the cat came into the room. Mick promptly took off and chased the cat up the stairs and into the bedroom where it took refuge on the top of a cabinet. Mick then turned his attention to the startled wife and leapt on to the bed to greet her joyfully, with a slobbery lick across her face; not a great experience, because his breath was rarely fragrant due to his habit of eating disgusting things he found in the field. Meantime his frantically wagging tail cleared the top of the bedside table. The offer to have him for a trial period was, not surprisingly, hastily withdrawn and Mick returned home.

Eventually my brother found a farmer on the outskirts of Frome who agreed to take the dog. He must have settled there, because we saw him no more, although we were apprehensive for some time that he might be returned.

After the Mick episode we were "dog-less" for a while and then my brother obtained a little black and white mongrel he named Spot. Her one and only misdemeanour was to go into our neighbour's farm one day and kill two of his hens. This was particularly embarrassing; at that time he was not on particularly good terms with this neighbour. The retribution on the poor bitch was so severe that she never went near poultry again. In due course Spot had a litter of puppies; one was retained, Whisky.

They lived on the farm for many years, and when they eventually died the next dog was a rather larger animal named Rupert. Early in his life, when he was in the kitchen, he had the misfortune to have some hot fat spilled on him, resulting in a bare patch on which hair never grew; but otherwise he was quite a handsome dog. He was the last of the farm dogs and moved with my brother and his wife when the farm was sold.

The number of cats varied, but generally there were two or three and their population was kept stable by drowning all unwanted kittens soon after they were born. They were not regarded as pets and were rarely given names, but just referred to as Puss or Tom, according to sex. They were kept for the sole purpose of

21

killing the rats and mice that would otherwise have infested the farm buildings and perhaps the house itself.

The cats were tolerated in the house, but not welcomed, as they were great thieves and would help themselves to any food within reach. They were always put out at night unless a resident mouse was suspected, in which case a cat would be left in to deal with it. The cats were fed once a day on stale bread soaked in leftover milk from the dairy, plus any kitchen scraps the dog hadn't eaten. They were expected to obtain the remainder of their sustenance from the mice they caught. The cats were generally lean and scrawny and often had torn ears or bitten faces from battles with the rats. At one time there was a large black and white feral tom that would not allow anyone near it. He would lie in wait in the fields for the occasional rabbit to supplement his diet. Unwary birds were fair game for all the cats and young poultry had to be protected from them.

When my brother and his wife took over the farm in the 1950s they were not so careful in reducing the number of kittens, with the result that the cat population steadily increased until there were about twenty, many of them feral. Arriving at the farm by car at night the headlights would shine on the eyes of cats scattered around the farmyard, which was quite a sight. When the farm was sold there was the problem of disposing of these cats as most of them were too wild to be approached. Eventually the services of the R.S.P.C.A. had to be sought; they brought special equipment to catch them, and so by the time the farm was pulled down all the cats had gone.

The farm was never without at least a couple of dozen hens that scratched around in the farmyard and the adjoining fields. They provided eggs for the family's use and a surplus to be sold on the milk round. It was a daily task to go and collect the eggs, which were not always in the nest boxes provided, but sometimes laid in out of the way places.

Chicks were hatched in the spring to replenish the stock and provide young cockerels to be fattened for Christmas. This was about the only time that ordinary people ate poultry; it was too expensive for other than special treats. In the 1930s, a young cockerel weighing about 5 lbs when made ready for the table, was the equivalent of about a third of a working man's weekly wage so it is no wonder it was considered a luxury meal.

My father and brother killed, plucked and gutted the poultry, and there would be feathers everywhere sometimes even invading the house. At busy times like Christmas there were too many cockerels to be dealt with at the farm and the job of plucking was given to a widow lady who I think was paid about one shilling for each bird. The widow had a mentally retarded son living with her who would hide when anyone came to the door, and then peep out to see who it was. He wore a cap indoors and out into which he tucked his long hair, which he would not allow to be cut. He was quite a bizarre sight, but quite amiable and harmless, and later on improved to the point where he was able to live a near normal life.

In addition to the Christmas poultry, the older hens were killed off when they ceased to lay and sold as "boilers": too tough to be roasted and needing to be boiled. These were much cheaper than the young cockerels, but not so cheap as to be suitable for an everyday meal.

As mentioned before, there was a small incubator at the farm that used a paraffin heater, but it was not all that reliable so most chicks were hatched by the old method of placing eggs under a hen. This meant that hatching could not be started until a hen became broody, which was generally in the spring. A nesting box was prepared in a segregated spot away from the other poultry, a dozen eggs were placed under her and the three-week incubation period commenced. If all went well generally eight to ten chicks were hatched, sometimes more. Very occasionally the hen would abandon the nest before the incubation period was over. If we didn't have a bird on the farm that could be persuaded to sit, someone was despatched on a bike to poultry-keeping neighbours to beg the loan of a broody hen. Sometimes these emergency measures worked, but not always, and then a brood was lost.

When the chicks hatched, generally over the period of a couple of days, they were first brought indoors and placed in a basket near the fire to dry out. Any loitering cats were swiftly ejected from the house. When hatching was completed the chicks were returned to the hen that was provided with a small pen and left to bring her brood up. When the young ones had grown sufficiently the females would join the hens and roam the farmyard whilst the young cockerels would be placed in a separate pen ready for fattening for Christmas.

An annoying chore, particularly on summer evenings, was to ensure that all the poultry were securely shut up for the night, safe from marauding foxes. Some hens were reluctant to go in whilst there was even a glimmer of daylight and any attempt to drive the last one in would cause such a commotion as to bring those in the houses out again. This could be extremely frustrating if an evening at the cinema had been planned and you had to wait for all the poultry to be shut in.

Towards the end of the war my brother decided to keep geese and obtained a goose and a gander. It was probably his intention to raise a flock, but this never happened. The few young ones that were raised did not thrive and probably succumbed to the cold wet conditions at the farm. However, the adults remained healthy and the goose laid an egg most days, which my brother had for his breakfast with home cured bacon, fried potatoes and mushrooms when available.

The gander rapidly established itself as the overlord and bully of the farm. He was a formidable bird and the hens and cockerels scattered before him. The cats were terrified of him and would look around cautiously before crossing the farmyard, and even the dog kept well clear of him. The calves when confronted by this hissing and wing flapping apparition would back away tossing their heads and mooing indignantly at having to give way.

Having conquered the farmyard the gander then turned his attention to humans. He would slyly approach from the rear and deliver a quite painful peck to the back of the leg before strutting off to honk and display to his admiring goose. He challenged visitors to such an extent that the postman refused to deliver mail and left it at one of the cottages at the end of the lane for us to collect. Female visitors would often wait at the end of the drive and call for assistance for someone to escort and protect them from assaults on their precious stockings.

My brother had been pretty tolerant of the gander's misdemeanours and was inclined to dismiss them as exaggeration until it rashly attacked him when he was shovelling pig manure into a wheelbarrow. Taken off balance by the bird's assault from the rear, he staggered forwards into the piled up wheelbarrow. Soon after this incident he decided that the gander was redundant and the following Sunday we had it for lunch, a little tough, but quite palatable. The goose lived on for quite a while still laying eggs regularly. Then early one summer morning my brother heard a commotion outside, a fox had the bird by the neck. He dashed out to scare the fox off, too late: the goose was eaten for dinner on Sunday.

When Father came to Frome in 1919/20 and started up a dairy business he bought a few cows. He took over a milk round from his brother Arthur and may possibly have bought cows from him. He never had more than about eight, but there was not sufficient pasture at Flint House even for this small number, so they were kept for most of the time in rented fields a half a mile or so from the farm. One field was off Robins Lane and another at the top of Egford Hill. There was a further one consisting of a long narrow strip of land alongside the road to Nunney.

At the end of this field was a small hillock from which the land fell away steeply down Nunney Hill and so provided splendid views across the countryside. It was shown on the map as Gibbet Hill as it was believed to be the site of a gibbet in the 16th or 17th century. Father said that when digging a hole for a post he came across a human bone, which he hastily reburied. It was also believed to be haunted, but nothing untoward was seen during Father's tenancy. All these fields were built upon in the 1950s and 60s and there is no trace of them now.

From time to time it was necessary to drive the cows along the roads from one field to another or for temporary location at the farm. This was a tedious business, because though there was very little traffic, and that slow moving, there were other problems. Once the cows were out of the field and on the road, which was not easily achieved, someone had to go in front to make sure all garden gates were shut. Otherwise a cow could quite easily wander into a neatly tended garden and cause havoc.

Father was usually at the back to keep them going and ideally there would be a third person to help at crossroads to ensure the cows did not divert from the correct route. The cows would amble along at their own pace sometimes wandering onto the pavement when they would often peer inquisitively into the windows of the little terrace houses or use a lamp post as a rubbing post. Needless to say the road would receive a liberal splattering of dung to mark the cows' progress. It was always a relief to get them to their destination without incident.

There was a continuous battle to keep the fences and hedges cattle proof, as this was long before the days of electric fencing. "Breakouts" did occur occasionally, often announced by the arrival at the farm of a boy on a bicycle bringing the unwelcome news that a cow, or cows, had got out and invaded someone's garden. Everyone had to turn out to get the animal back. Not an easy task as cows could move quickly if they wished and were naturally reluctant to be turned away from fodder more tasty than the grass in their field. One evening a cow broke through a fence and onto the road, and though this was not used much in those days it could have been a serious incident, but fortunately wasn't. Apart from frightening a passing cyclist, who was alarmed to see a large cow emerge from the gloom in front of him, no harm was done.

One or two men from a nearby pub were summoned and they rounded up the cow and secured it in a field until morning. They knew to whom the cow belonged, and Father was out of pocket only to the extent of the cost of a round of drinks next time he visited the pub. If the incident had been reported to the police he would have been summoned and fined.

All the cows had names and would respond if called, there was also an established order of precedence. The "boss" was a large red cow with formidable horns called Star — she had a white mark on her forehead roughly in the shape of a star. The others had names like Rose, Blossom, and Cowslip, until finally at the end of the pecking order was a small nervous brown and white cow called Daisy. When driven from field to field they walked in strict order of precedence and any cow that attempted to push in front of the boss cow was soon put in her place.

The cows spent all of their time outside and were never brought in. Father milked them in the open and carried a little three-legged stool from one to the other. The only shelter they got was from the trees in the hedgerows, but they were obviously hardy animals and seemed to thrive on their outdoor life.

They fed exclusively on grass in the summer and hay in the winter plus occasionally a handful of cow cake when they were being milked. The yield of milk per animal was considerably less than obtained nowadays since the improved breeding and feeding methods. In fact Father did not obtain sufficient milk from his cows for his milk round and bought extra supplies from other smallholders.

The cows were generally very amiable animals except when they had calves and then they were very protective and quite aggressive. I found this out when a very small boy; I ran after a young calf, wanting to play with it, and was bowled over by its mother. I might have suffered some injury if Father had not driven the cow off by throwing his milking stool at it.

Heifer calves were weaned and brought up to add to Father's small herd or to replace old cows that no longer yielded sufficient milk. When a calf was taken away it was upsetting for the cow; the distressed mother made its feelings known by loud bellowing for a day or two. This would often continue through the night, which was unpopular with the residents of nearby houses. Next morning when Father went to the field he would get grumbled at about disturbed sleep.

The calves were brought up at the farm and kept in the paddock until big enough to be with the other cows. They could sometimes be a nuisance if they got through the fence into the next field and had to be brought back. Chasing them was useless as they could run very fast and seemed to delight in evading capture. The best ploy was to tempt them back by offering something they liked, such as cow cake.

Periodically visiting inspectors would arrive unannounced to test the quality of the milk being sold and take samples from the milkman's bucket. Father's milk always passed the test, but one or two milkmen were prosecuted for selling milk with too high a water content and in due course would appear at the local Petty Session. Unbelieving magistrates would listen to stories of milk buckets having lids left off momentarily when a sudden downpour of rain occurred. Normally a fine was imposed and a warning given. In a small town like Frome there were still quite a number of milkmen vying with each other for custom.

Once a year rivalry was put to one side for a milkmen's outing and a charabanc would be hired for an afternoon's trip to the seaside at Weymouth or Weston-super-Mare.

My father bought a pony soon after he moved to Frome around 1919/20 and started up a dairy business. It was used to pull a milk float for door-to-door deliveries. The pony, Jimmy, was a sturdy animal, brown in colour; it served my father well, gave no trouble and needed little attention other than the occasional visit to the blacksmith for new shoes. Right up to Father's death in 1939 it patiently pulled the milk float every day.

My earliest memories were of Jimmy and there is a photograph taken about 1923 of me, a small infant, perched on his back. Mother was so proud of this photograph that she had a huge enlargement framed and hung on the wall.

Jimmy had a regular routine. Early in the morning he was harnessed up to the float and driven to the field where the cows were kept. The paddock at the farm was not big enough for our cows so they were kept in rented fields half a mile or so away. Arriving at the field Jimmy was left to graze whilst Father milked the cows. When milking was finished the milk was poured into a churn carried on the float, and Father was ready to start delivering.

There were no such refinements as pasteurisation or even cooling the milk in those days, it was just strained through butter muslin to remove any bits of grass or straw and then loaded onto the float. The earliest deliveries of milk were still warm from the cow, and the customers quite liked this, as they knew the milk was fresh.

The round consisted mainly of rows of terrace houses interspersed with a few larger and detached ones. Milk was not bottled in those days and Father ladled it out of the bucket into the customer's jug. At some of the houses the jug was left just inside the door or on the dresser, the milk was poured in and a saucer put over it to keep the cat off. The few pennies for payment were left ready for collection, sometimes inside the jug. In those more trusting days the doors were often unlocked so that tradesmen could be left to make their deliveries without disturbing the customer. Generally, only small quantities of milk were bought, half pints were the norm as it was mainly only used in tea. Working people did not generally eat breakfast cereals. Some of the bigger houses had more milk, perhaps a pint or even a quart a day. The latter were considered very good customers indeed and would be rewarded with a free pot of cream at Christmas.

Jimmy knew the round perfectly and needed little guidance. He would wander slowly along the road, there was almost a complete absence of other traffic in those days, stopping outside the houses of any customers that sometimes gave him titbits: a piece of toast or a carrot. There were two pubs en route at which Father would stop for a quick drink and a chat. Jimmy knew this and would pull in by these unbidden and wait for Father to emerge. Another stop was at a small market garden, the owner of which, Mr. Elton, kept a few cows. Father bought milk from him to replenish the churn on the float to complete the remainder of his round.

The round would be finished by about one o'clock and then Father would return to the farm for his dinner. Jimmy would be unharnessed and turned out in the paddock for a couple of hours, only for the process to be repeated later in the afternoon: the cows had to be milked again and some more deliveries made. It would be early evening before all was finished and Father could come back to the farm. Then Jimmy was let loose in the paddock for the night.

At haymaking time Jimmy was sometimes needed to pull a hay rake or cart, but these were brief interludes in his daily routine.

Jimmy stayed outside in all weathers and rarely came into the farmyard seeking shelter. He was nearly always ready to be caught to be harnessed up; just occasionally he would be skittish, and toss his head and gallop away, and had to be coaxed with a piece of bread or apple. These displays of temperament usually occurred when Father was late and gave rise to a great deal of bad language.

This routine continued until Father's sudden death in 1939. Jimmy then became redundant as my brother incorporated Father's round into his own and used a van to make the deliveries. The pony became bored with his idle life and quite often came and stood in the farmyard obviously hoping to be harnessed up to the float.

Once, taking advantage of the open back door he came right into the house and as there wasn't space to turn him round he had, with some difficulty, to be persuaded to back right down the passage and out into the farmyard. On another occasion he pushed over a pen housing small chickens and watched with apparent interest, and perhaps amusement, our frantic efforts to catch them.

Eventually my brother sold him to a local farmer who was able to use him for tasks about his farm. Jimmy was with us for about 20 years, he was missed, but the many changes brought about by the war rather overshadowed his absence.

The cows continued to be kept until my father's death in 1939, but were then sold, as my brother could not look after them and run his quite large milk round as well. During the war years the milkmen combined their individual rounds into one to save labour and reduce transport costs.

After the war however my brother gave up milk delivery and went into farming. He bought cows and acquired a couple of fields and also a milking shed. Cows were now milked inside, as much higher standards of cleanliness were demanded in post war years. He never installed milking machines and milked by hand until he retired in the 1970s. One thing that had not changed was the need to drive cows from field to field, but now along increasingly busier roads.

On his retirement the cows were sold, the farmhouse was pulled down and the fields became building plots. It was the end of an era. On part of one of his fields he built a bungalow as a retirement home for him and his wife, but he continued to keep poultry and one or two calves for several years.

CHAPTER
ONE

1939

I was 17 years old in September 1939 when war was declared, and would be 18 at the end of the year. I had been working as a clerk at the Longleat Estate Forestry Office in Horningsham since January of that year when I left school, and as Sunday was my only complete day off I normally stayed in bed until late.

On Sunday September 3rd I roused myself, and got up in time to hear the special radio announcement by the Prime Minister at 11a.m. I remember very clearly standing in our living room and hearing the declaration that we were at war with Germany. My mother wept, because she had two sons of military age, and my father tried to comfort her. For myself I had few misgivings and it all seemed rather exciting.

The announcement did not come as any surprise, as it had been obvious for some weeks that war was likely. Everyone had already been issued with a gas mask, contained in a brown cardboard box with a sling enabling it to be carried on the shoulder. We were supposed to keep them with us at all times, and initially this was done, but as nothing seemed to be happening the gas masks were generally left at home.

Instructions had been issued about blackout requirements, and most households had their blackout curtains ready to be put up when war was eventually declared. A rationing system was in place, but had little impact for the first few months of the war.

My job required me to cycle seven miles to work over a very hilly route; it normally took about 45 minutes. My starting wage was £1 a week, which rose to £1.2.6d after three months. For this I calculated the wages for the hundred or so work force and made up the pay packets. As I was the only clerk, I also did all the general office work, such as producing invoices for the sale of timber.

The only perquisite was the gift at Christmas of either a pair of rabbits or a brace of pheasants according to your status in the firm. The lower grades, say labourers, received rabbits, and the higher echelons like managers were given pheasants. The two Christmases that I was in the Horningsham office I received rabbits — an indication of my status.

Very shortly after the declaration of war we had within our family a tragedy when my father died. Early in October he contracted pleurisy, which turned to pneumonia, and within two weeks he died at the early age of 53. The years he had spent working as a miner had affected his lungs and they were not strong enough to withstand an attack of these pernicious diseases. In 1939 there were not the drugs available to combat such maladies.

Apart from the sadness of our bereavement life went on much as normal during the remainder of 1939. We had to cope with blackout restrictions, and get used to avoiding lampposts and falling over kerbstones whilst walking at night in a blacked out town. On the farm we were used to getting round in the dark.

There were soldiers billeted in or just outside Frome and they could be seen in the streets and pubs. Some of my schoolmates, a little older than me, had joined the Territorials. I remember going to a social in the church hall on the Saturday before war was declared, and seeing them resplendent in their uniforms. There was dancing; a favourite tune called "South of the Border" will always remind me of that night.

The Territorials were soon whisked away and we did not see them again for several years, as they served overseas. Most, but not all, returned safely after the war.

Conscription had started earlier in the year, but I was too young to be called up. Initially, only a fairly narrow age range was affected, probably something like 19–21-year-olds, but as the war progressed eventually all men from 18 to about 40 were liable for call up, unless they were in a reserved occupation.

Women, too, were directed into the forces or to essential war work.

In November 1939 I met Eileen Palmer and we started going out together: as it was called at that time. She lived at the opposite end of the town, so I had a two-mile walk through the blackout each time I called for her. This involved ascending and descending some formidable hills; at the time I thought nothing of it.

By the end of the year, the war had made little impact on us at Frome, apart from the inconvenience of the blackout. This period was often referred to as the "phoney war".

Our Christmas was somewhat subdued, because of our recent bereavement, but there was one bright spot on Christmas Eve when my brother walked in carrying a large live goose that he had won in a raffle at the local pub. Too late to be eaten on Christmas Day, it was saved for a future occasion.

The war had affected my sister and her husband in that they were required to have an evacuee, even though they had a twelve-month-old baby of their own. They were lucky to get a well-behaved boy from a school evacuated to Frome. He stayed with them for the rest of the war, and in fact kept in touch with my sister for the rest of her life.

CHAPTER
TWO

1940

The first four or five months of this year followed much the same pattern as 1939, as far as the war was concerned. It made little impact on our lives in Frome; there were a few restrictions arising from rationing.

At Easter, however, I suffered a personal upset in every meaning of the word when I had a cycling accident. Unwisely, I was carrying, slung over my handlebars, a canvas bag in which there had been milk bottles. Whilst going down the hill at Broadway the bag caught in my front wheel. I was projected over the handlebars onto the road and knocked out. I regained consciousness to find myself sitting in someone's front room, bleeding profusely from a lacerated face, and with two missing front teeth. The local hospital patched me up and I returned home heavily bandaged and very sore.

This event gave rise to Eileen's first visit to my home at the farm. Accompanied by a mutual friend, she brought me grapes, and saw me with a bandaged face lying on my sick bed.

Shortly afterwards she was invited to Sunday tea, when the rest of the family — my brother, sister and her husband — assembled to meet her. Mother's best crockery and the very best white tablecloth were on display. After the meal, when the table was cleared, Eileen, attempting to be helpful, took off the cloth and shook the crumbs into the hearth. This fireplace had a large straight chimney; it had been known for birds to fall down it and fly around the room in their sooty state, hotly pursued by the cat. It also had a very fierce draught, and the cloth was suddenly sucked up the flue. My mother smiled politely, and said it was quite all right, as if it was of no consequence that her best tablecloth had been reduced from its white, pristine state to a filthy, soot stained rag. It was a very sorry sight when retrieved. Goodness knows what she really thought.

From about May 1940, there were dramatic changes in the war: the Germans invaded France and swept all before them. There followed the Dunkirk evacuation of British troops, the war in the air, and the bombing of British cities. Repercussions from these great events were felt even in rural backwaters. Some of the troops evacuated from Dunkirk were billeted in and around Frome and one of the hotels, The Portway, was requisitioned to become an Army Headquarters.

I still have clear memories of the following events that I witnessed at that time:

— Whilst measuring timber in Longleat woods, I looked up and saw several squadrons of German bombers, perhaps fifty or sixty aircraft, flying in

41

perfect formation. I wondered what chance we had if German aircraft could fly with such impunity and unchallenged in broad daylight. I did hear afterwards that British fighters intercepted them before they reached their target, Bristol. Although several were shot down the aircraft factory at Bristol was heavily bombed.

— Getting a glimpse of a German aircraft emerging from low cloud and disappearing back into it. The sound was quite distinctive, quite unlike British aircraft.

— Visiting a pub in the village of Corsley to see minor damage caused by a small bomb that dropped nearby. A bomb fragment pierced the back of one of the seats; fortunately it was unoccupied at the time.

— Cycling home from work one evening, and seeing a bomb disposal squad digging out an unexploded bomb in a field adjacent to the road.

— On my way to work each day, seeing the progress being made on a deep, defensive ditch that was being dug across country in preparation for the expected invasion. Holes were cut into each road that crossed the route of the ditch, so iron rails, which were stacked at the roadside, could be slotted into place to form a tank barrier.

— Concrete block-houses (pillboxes) were rapidly built at strategic points, from which machine gun and rifle fire could be directed at invading troops. Many of these pillboxes can still be found in secluded spots with little sign of deterioration after more than sixty years.

— Watching long poles being erected vertically in a large open field at Longleat to prevent it being used as a landing ground by enemy gliders.

— Seeing Longleat House being used by a boarding school evacuated from Bath. The Marquis continued to live there, in a part that had been converted into a self-contained flat.

— One night at the farm, hearing gunfire overhead when a British night fighter intercepted a German aircraft. On going outside, we saw a glow in the distance that may, or may not have been an aircraft shot down.

— Seeing signposts removed from all roads, even minor country roads. The intention was to frustrate enemy parachutists seeking to discover where they had landed. This was of little inconvenience to local people who knew all the roads in their own neighbourhood, but it was a great nuisance to visiting motorists.

— At the same time, location signs were removed from railway stations. Travelling at night, when arriving at a blacked out country station, it was difficult for passengers to know where they were. They were dependent on the porter calling out the name in an intelligible manner.

The formation of the Home Guard or LDV (Local Defence Volunteers) as it was generally called, did have an impact on our lives, as my brother Cliff and my brother-in-law Ernie were quick to join. I decided not to. My mind was set on joining the RAF; which I expected to be able to do fairly soon, but it was a further nine months before I was accepted by that service.

At the start there were no uniforms for the Home Guard, and volunteers merely had armbands to distinguish them from other civilians. The issue of khaki denim uniforms soon followed, and shortly after each member was issued with a rifle and five rounds of ammunition. The rifles had been in store for many years and were well greased, and had to be cleaned before use. My brother did his on the lawn, and took the immaculate rifle upstairs to be kept in the bedroom ready for use. The five rounds of ammunition were kept in a bedside cabinet.

Drills were frequent; and my brother would sally forth, complete with rifle and ammunition, for training either at the local Drill Hall or somewhere outside.

At night, guards were mounted at what were considered vulnerable or strategic spots. The water reservoir was one, as it was situated at the top of a hill, and commanded views across the countryside. After a spell of night duty my brother had to return to the farm to do a day's work.

In September it was thought that invasion was imminent, and one evening the troops stationed in and around Frome were sent at short notice to the south coast. I remember being at the cinema that evening; the programme was interrupted several times by notices flashed on the screen telling members of the various regiments — e.g. the Grenadier Guards, the Leicester Regiment — to report back to Barracks immediately.

The Home Guard was put on the highest state of alert and manned their various posts. We were all apprehensive, and scanned the skies anxiously expecting to see German parachutists descending. My brother was there all night, and whilst the alert continued into the morning he had to be released from duty in order to milk his cows. In the event nothing happened, though there were rumours that an invasion had been attempted and driven back, but later we learned that this was not so.

My brother and brother-in-law served in the Home Guard for the remainder of the war. Ernie was eventually commissioned and became a Lieutenant, and Cliff was promoted to the rank of Corporal.

A bigger impact on our lives resulted from the heavy bombing of London in September. As mentioned earlier, my sister had an evacuee who came from Bow in East London, and his mother and father had been to Frome several times to visit him.

One night in September, the bombing was so intense that next morning his parents, together with a sister and her husband, packed into their car and fled to Frome. They arrived unannounced at the farm, as neither my sister nor we had telephones. My mother managed to find beds for them in the farmhouse. There were two spare bedrooms: one a little more than a storeroom, neither was in very good decorative order.

The conditions must have been something of a shock to these city-dwellers. In London they lived in a modern house with gas, electricity, inside toilet, bathroom and kitchen with constant hot water. The farm had none of these things. There was one cold-water tap in the dairy, and water for washing had to be heated in a kettle. The toilet was outside, and could only be flushed by carrying a bucket of water to it. Oil lamps and candles were the only source of light. Such heating as there was came from coal fires, and there were none upstairs.

The men had to return to London for their work after a day or two, but the wives stayed on and settled down to rural life. In fact, they stayed for the rest of the war, just returning to London for short periods from time to time. They adapted well to the lack of amenities, and learnt to do their cooking on paraffin stoves.

They also got used to traversing the very muddy lane, which was the only approach to the farm, and at night was in complete darkness. There were problems, of course. One evening early in their stay they decided to go to the pictures. There was no one else in the house, and they realised they had not been shown how to put out the lamp. Rather than risk leaving it lit in an empty house, they abandoned their planned trip and stayed in.

On Boxing Day, I wondered when I would have Christmas at the farm again. I was pretty certain I would be in one of the services within a few weeks.

It was to be five years before I was home for Christmas again.

CHAPTER
THREE

1941

In this year, the war changed my life completely. Within a few months I was thousands of miles away from my home in Frome, and engaged in the type of work previously unknown to me.

Early in the year I applied to join the RAF; as I said before, I fancied this service more than the other two. In February, I received a notice asking me to attend an RAF recruiting office in Bristol for Attestation. It advised me not to give up my job, because even if accepted it would probably be several weeks before I was required. The notice also said to come prepared for an overnight stay in case this was necessary.

I duly reported to the office in Bristol on March 5th, accompanied by a Frome lad I met on the train and knew slightly. There then followed some form filling and a thorough medical examination in a cold room with the minimum of privacy. I was graded A1, except for vision, which was A2. The latter grading ruled out flying duties, which, though I didn't know it at the time, may well have saved my life: as the war progressed there were very heavy casualties among flying personnel.

The A1 grading made me ineligible for clerical or store keeping duties for which I would otherwise have been most suited. I was in a quandary; I was fairly ignorant about RAF trades. Which trade should I apply for?

The Recruiting Sergeant seemed very helpful, and suggested I might like to be an Armourer. He assured me it was a most interesting and useful trade, and required a high level of intelligence, which he was sure I possessed. I succumbed to his persuasive talk and signed a declaration agreeing to be trained as an Armourer. Once he had my signature, the Sergeant became considerably less helpful. He told me curtly, because of the shortage of recruits in this trade, I would be required immediately for service and there could be no question of me returning home. When I drew his attention to the paragraph in my notification about not giving up my job, he just shrugged and said, "Exigencies of the service". This was a phrase I was to hear constantly during my time in the RAF.

I was able to have a few words with the Frome lad with whom I had travelled. He was returning home as he was not required for immediate service, and kindly agreed to call on my mother and break the bad news to her. There was no other way to contact her.

Like many bearers of bad news he did not receive a very warm welcome. My mother rather crossly asked why he was allowed home when her son was not. I do not think "Exigencies of the service" would have been a satisfactory response.

Those required for immediate service, about twenty or thirty of us, were assembled in one room and then accompanied by a Corporal taken to Temple Meads railway station, where we were put on a train to Penarth — a seaside town near Cardiff. By then it was early afternoon and we were all hungry. Fortunately, we were able to get a snack and a drink at the station while we waited for a train.

We knew Cardiff had been heavily bombed a day or two before, and wondered if there would be a follow up raid.

RAF Penarth

At Penarth we were taken to our accommodation: rooms in a large requisitioned house. There were five or six men to a room, which had beds and blankets, but virtually nothing else, and certainly no heating. We had little time to study our accommodation before we were rushed off to the RAF canteen for our evening meal. This was my first RAF meal; it was awful, but I was so hungry that I ate it anyway. It consisted of a plate of boiled potatoes, over which had been poured melted cheese, followed by a piece of cake and rather watery custard.

Then it was back to the billet to chat to my roommates and get some sleep. Two of them came from the same village and were friends. They hit on the idea of pulling their beds together and sharing their blankets. This meant they had double the blanket thickness, and as it was cold in our billet I thought it was very sensible. When the orderly Sergeant came round in the morning, he was not at all pleased to find two recruits tucked up in bed together, and made it quite clear that this was not done in the RAF. I was naïve enough to wonder why.

The next morning we were taken to a large store to receive our uniforms and other necessaries. Firstly we received a kit bag. Then we queued to pass along a counter behind which were store men, who at a bewildering speed slung items of clothing and equipment at us, while shouting out the nomenclature in what seemed almost like a foreign language, e.g. coats, great, blue grey, Airman size 8. We were asked our sizes of things like boots and shirts, but otherwise the store man used his judgement with varying degrees of success.

The items had to be stuffed into the kit bag at full speed in order to keep up with the queue, and also not to attract the attention of the supervising Sergeant who was constantly bellowing at us to keep moving, and pointing out quite unnecessarily that this was not a fashion show. At the end I had a bag full of items, and hoped that I had been issued with all that I had signed for.

We returned to our billet to try on our new apparel, with some guidance from a Corporal. He also gave us each a large piece of brown paper and string so that we could send our civilian clothes home. I had never made up a parcel before, but by using yards and yards of string I hoped it would be secure enough to travel to

Frome without shedding its contents on the way — there was no sellotape in those days.

Indeed it did arrive safely, causing my mother to break into tears when she unwrapped it and saw her son's garments that had been returned so peremptorily and with no advance warning.

On checking through my uniform I made the disquieting discovery that one pair of boots had one rubber sole and one leather one. My roommates confirmed that this was not another mysterious RAF practice, and that both boot soles should be of the same material. This posed a quandary, because I was reluctant to return to the clothing store and confront the belligerent Sergeant who had made clear his low opinion of recruits. On the other hand, I didn't see how I could continue to wear odd boots.

Plucking up courage, I returned to the store where I was received with undisguised irritation. When in quavering voice I explained my problem and handed over the offending boots, the Sergeant asked me if my other pair of boots were the same. He obviously thought I was stupid enough to get them mixed up. I assured him that they were not. With very poor grace he changed them, lamenting loudly about the quality of present day recruits who were not alert enough to spot mismatched boots at the time of issue.

I returned to my billet and learned that we were to parade after lunch to see if we needed haircuts. I felt quite smug when I heard this; I had had a haircut only a few days before in anticipation of such a check. I need not have bothered, because at the inspection, without hesitation, the Sergeant said, "Haircut", as he did for almost all the recruits.

We proceeded to the RAF barber, but now we were in uniform we were required to march. We obviously did not do this to the satisfaction of the Corporal in charge: he likened us to a herd of cows going to be milked. We emerged from the barber shorn to the point of baldness, and wondering what further indignity would be heaped on us.

The next day we were assembled to hear our posting details. I was delighted to be told I was to go to RAF Melksham, only about fifteen miles from my home in Frome. There I would first of all do a three-week Recruit Training Course — generally known as square bashing — followed by a six-week Bomb Armourers Course.

I should explain, pre-war there was just the single trade of Armourer. When the war started there was a great need for many more Armourers, and it was decided to split the trade in two — "bombs" and "guns" — each with a training period of six to eight weeks. In this way double the number would be "trained". The pre-war Armourers Course took about six months, whereas the combined, separate trades of Bomb and Gun totalled little more than three months.

In an attempt to make up the deficiency, longer hours were worked and certain aspects omitted. It worked reasonably well, but sometimes Bomb Armourers were posted to RAF stations where most of the work related to guns, and vice versa. Then it was a case of learning on the job, which was not an ideal situation when dealing with lethal materials such as ammunition and explosives. Any such fears would be dismissed by the commonly used phrase, "Don't you know there is a war on".

That evening was to be our last at Penarth. We packed our belongings in our new kit bags, which now bore our names and RAF numbers.

An entrepreneur among the permanent staff had neatly printed these. This Airman had been a sign writer in civilian life and had with him the tools of the trade. He went to all the recruits and offered to mark their kit bags for a small charge of about a shilling (5p). This was almost half a day's pay for the recruits, but most accepted. The enterprising Airman earned more from this activity than from the RAF.

The next morning at the railway station, we stood in line facing the edge of the platform ready to get on the train, with our kit bags in front of us. An officer told us to put them behind us, because a line of white kit bags could attract the attention of a low flying aircraft. Eventually the train came along and we boarded it without hindrance from enemy aircraft, and so were on our way to Melksham.

As we passed through the outskirts of Cardiff we saw the damage caused by enemy bombing that had taken place a few days earlier.

CHAPTER
FOUR

1941 — RAF Melksham

We arrived at Melksham late afternoon and an RAF lorry was waiting to take our kit bags to the camp. Since, so far, our experience of the RAF suggested that a lorry would not be provided unless absolutely essential, it seemed likely that the camp was a long way from the railway station. We set off marching as best we knew how, and did not attract comment from the accompanying Corporal who knew that we would soon be receiving attention from the Drill Sergeant.

It was indeed a good distance to the camp. We met groups of Airmen going into town who shouted out unkind comments:

"You shouldn't have joined!"

"You are going the wrong way!" etc.

Eventually we got there, and after being counted, presumably to see if anyone had deserted on route from the station, we were ushered into a shed. Here a Sergeant gave each of us a knife, fork and spoon, and also a large white china mug bearing the RAF crest. He impressed on us that these items were now our personal property and we would keep them for the rest of our service in the RAF.

We were then taken to our billets at the opposite end of the camp from the entrance. We could hardly believe our eyes. We were shown into a large aircraft hangar, which had been divided into about twenty bays by rows of sand bags piled chest high. Each bay contained a dozen or so beds: the hangar accommodated over two hundred Airmen. There was no sign of washing or toilet facilities, and we found later that these were in a separate building about fifty yards away.

We were directed into a bay to take possession of empty beds, and at that point I dropped my mug. It landed on the concrete floor and shattered into a dozen pieces. The sound of the crash was greeted by raucous cheers from all the Airmen in the hangar. I learned later that this was the custom whenever a mug was dropped. The Sergeant who only a few minutes before had given me this mug, assuring me it was to be mine for the rest of my service, almost exploded with rage. In strident tones he made it clear that a replacement mug would not be issued, that the war effort was being impaired by such carelessness, and that I would have to manage as best I could.

I was devastated, and panic stricken. Frightening thoughts raced through my mind, "I had nothing to drink out of, so what should I do? I might die of thirst, but surely the RAF would not let that happen. No, but that Sergeant might!"

I pulled myself together to find that we were to be marched to the cookhouse for supper, and I was sadly aware that everyone had a mug except me. Somehow I managed over the next few days, thanks to the kindness of my fellow Airmen, and by drinking out of a variety of receptacles. Eventually, I was able to get into town and buy a mug, a tin one.

The next three weeks were pretty uneventful. I got used to the primitive conditions in which we lived, though I must admit I did not take kindly to having to use cold water for shaving — no electric razors in those days. I had been brought up on a farm with no gas, electricity or hot water system and with an outside toilet, so perhaps it was not so much of a shock for me as for some others. Anyway, I was nineteen, fairly fit and pretty resilient so I was confident that I could manage.

During these three weeks we drilled on the parade ground, and were shouted at by the Sergeants who were endeavouring to teach us to march smartly, do arms drill and perform the various manoeuvres that the Drill Book required. Most of the Sergeants' invective was directed at the poor unfortunates who seemed incapable of swinging their arms properly when marching. I think I escaped pretty lightly as I did not find the various drill movements too difficult, although I did drop my rifle once, which did not exactly endear me to the Sergeant.

Now I had a permanent address, at least for three weeks, I could write letters and hope for a reply. The big bonus was that we had Sundays off, and we were allowed out of camp from early morning until midnight, or 23.59 as the RAF liked to call it. On my first Sunday I managed to get home by bus in time for lunch, and then in the evening I cycled back to camp and parked my bike in an air raid shelter ready for the next weekend.

I was delighted to be able to return home every weekend, to see Eileen and my family. They were able to see me in my ill-fitting uniform and clumsy boots, and hear about my experiences since my previous leave. It was good to have some home cooking again, and I generally returned to camp with a cake or pie to eat during the week.

Before the three weeks of "square bashing" finished, I had one further brush with the Sergeant who had taken such offence at the breaking of my mug. Towards the end of the course he gave us a lecture on hygiene. When he was telling us how to look after our feet he suddenly asked how we cut our toenails. I brightly answered, "With scissors!"

I was soon made aware that this was not the answer he wanted; he took a deep breath and looked upwards as if seeking divine help. "Of course you use scissors," he shouted. "I didn't think you bit them off you clot!"

It turned out that he wanted to know what shape we cut our toenails: round across the top or square. I felt like pointing out that if his question had been framed more precisely he would have got a more helpful answer, but I thought he would not take kindly to such criticism and wisely remained silent.

At the end of the three weeks basic training we started almost straight away on six weeks technical training, aimed at turning us into competent Bomb Armourers. We moved from the hanger to more comfortable quarters in huts. This was the type of accommodation I was to have for most of my service in the RAF.

Each hut housed about thirty Airmen, and in a separate building nearby were washing facilities and toilets. Hot water was sometimes available, but not always. Each bed had a shelf overhead for the Airman's possessions, which had to be stacked neatly. The bed had to be made up each morning and the blankets folded up in the approved fashion, there were no sheets.

During the six weeks we had a series of lectures about explosives, bombs, flares, fuses . . . plus practice in fitting bombs to aircraft fuselages housed in a nearby hangar. The Instructors were generally good, and all had practical experience in the skills they were teaching. One particular lecture still remains in my mind as it probably does for most other trainees. The Instructor was a quietly spoken and rather phlegmatic character. He was showing us how to fit a fuse fitted with a delayed action, anti-handling device to a bomb: a device that would cause the bomb to explode if the enemy attempted to remove it.

"I want you to pay particular attention to this, because if you get it wrong when dealing with a real bomb you, and anyone in the vicinity, will be killed." He got our undivided attention.

Fortunately, in all my time in the service, I never had to deal with this type of fuse, but I did hear that it caused a major accident at one squadron and was subsequently discontinued.

At the start of the course we were told about a superior grade of Armourer, called a Fitter Armourer, who had a higher rate of pay. They were employed on work requiring greater skills: repairs and modifications to equipment. We were told we would be tested to see if we showed aptitude for this kind of work, and if so would be sent on a further three months course to train as Fitter Armourers.

I was not over optimistic about my chances of being accepted. I remembered my dismal performance at woodwork classes at school. My total output was a spade scraper that broke after my father used it two or three times, and a small bookrack that fell apart when books were put into it. Unenthusiastically, I went to the workshop to be tested.

We were each given a piece of mild steel and told that from this we should make an adjustable spanner. We were given instructions and provided with all necessary tools and left to get on with it.

For several afternoons I toiled away using hacksaws, files, screw cutting tools . . . and acquired blisters on my hands, and a few cuts, as a result. At the end of the allotted time I had produced something that, at a cursory glance, did indeed look like the required item, even though the jaws were uneven and gaped. However, it suffered from one great disadvantage for an adjustable spanner — it would not adjust.

One at a time we went into the office to show our spanner to a grey-haired warrant officer who looked as if he had been in the RAF forever, or since Pontius was a pilot, as the saying went. He looked sadly at my offering over which I had toiled so long, and then, after the briefest of examinations, tossed it into the waste bin.

"Never mind, lad," he said kindly, "you are probably good at other things." I sensed that he said it with little conviction.

When the course ended I was graded AC2 (Aircraftman Second Class) Bomb Armourer, and had a rise in pay of sixpence a day. That brought my new daily rate up to three shillings, or twenty-one shillings a week, £1.05. Half of this was deducted and paid to my mother, because she was a widow, and the RAF also made her an allotment. I, therefore, only received 10s 6d (52½p) per week.

We were all given a week's leave. I was not to return, but to report to RAF Andover. I left Melksham with some regrets, because I had been able to get home every weekend and I rightly surmised this was not likely to happen again.

After my leave I caught a train from Frome to Andover, to be told that the RAF camp was three or four miles out of town. Fortunately, an RAF lorry turned up and I got a lift to the camp.

RAF Andover

After going through all the administrative procedures and being given a billet, I found my way to the Station Armoury and reported to the Sergeant in charge. He was a regular who had been in the RAF since long before the war — like most of the ground crew NCOs.

He had not heard of the grade of Bomb Armourer; in his experience Armourers dealt with all aspects of armourments, and there was no specialisation. He went on to explain that there were no bombs at Andover; the aircraft they had were Blenheims, used in Army cooperation, such as reconnaissance for Army units. The aircraft carried guns and flares and very occasionally practice bombs. He wasn't discouraging in any way, and assured me I would be all right if I just watched what the other Armourers were doing and learnt from them. So this is what I did, and acted as a sort of plumber's mate. It was a novelty for me to see real aircraft on the ground and get into them.

Enemy aircraft had attacked the camp a few weeks before, and there had been some damage and fatalities, and this was still the subject of much conversation.

The camp was quite widely dispersed; my billet, the Cookhouse and the Armoury were some distance from each other, which was a nuisance for me, as I did not have a bike I had a lot of walking. The accommodation, in huts similar to those at Melksham, was quite comfortable and my roommates were friendly.

I remember a rather strange Airman in my hut who would sometimes go outside and with a piece of chalk, draw chickens on the path and then throw crumbs to them. I was told he was awaiting medical assessment, which did not surprise me.

After only a few weeks at Andover there was a bombshell for me: I was to be posted overseas immediately after seven days embarkation leave. My destination was not disclosed; I was just told it was Draft No. 191. Hurriedly I got clearance from the camp and went home. I was not able to enjoy the full week's leave, because after five days I received a telegram telling me to report back to camp immediately. Eileen saw me off at the station and as the train pulled out I wondered sadly if I would ever see Frome again. The war news was at its blackest and I did not know where I was going or for how long.

I returned to RAF Andover as instructed and was issued with my travel documents. First thing next morning, on the 1st July, I was able to set off for the Embarkation Unit at West Kirby, near Liverpool. This involved a train journey from Andover to London Waterloo, underground to Euston, train to Liverpool and finally local train to West Kirby. This was a completely new experience for me as I had never been to London, or further north than Bristol. Of course, I had to carry my kitbag, which was cumbersome in crowded trains. Eventually, I arrived at West Kirby station to find I was one of about two hundred Airmen on the platform. We were marched to the camp, which was more than a mile away, and still carrying our heavy kitbags.

RAF West Kirby

I was at West Kirby for about five days, and during that time we had medical and dental examinations, and several kit parades. We were issued with khaki tropical kit including a topee, and our anti gas clothing and steel helmets were taken away. The issue of tropical kit made us sure we were going to the Middle East, whilst the topee made us think of India.

One of our number was late on parade and joined the wrong queue. He was issued with clothing for Iceland and was puzzled that his garments were so different from ours. He managed to get it sorted out after a hurried return to the clothing store.

Very early on the morning of Saturday, July 5th, we paraded again and were taken to the station to catch the train to Liverpool. We marched through the town to the docks, again carrying all our kit.

CHAPTER
FIVE

1941

S.S. Ruanhine

We were able to see the bomb damage, caused by the frequent raids on Liverpool, but fortunately there were none while we were there. When we reached the docks we boarded our ship, the S.S. Ruanhine.

Before the war the Ruanhine had been used to carry meat from New Zealand to Great Britain, and had been requisitioned and converted to a troop carrier. Its maximum speed was said to be about twelve knots, so it was always likely to be the slowest boat in the convoy. It was armed with two naval guns in the stern, and a couple of machine guns. Members of the ship's crew, who did gun drill from time to time, manned these.

Once aboard we were informed that our destination was Canada. We were ushered down two flights of steps to our accommodation, and were pretty appalled at what we saw. We were in one of the holds of the ship. At the time I noted it to be about 160 × 70 feet, into which were crammed nearly six hundred men. The only furniture was a mess table where we would eat, and forms to sit on. Overhead hooks had been fixed to the beams so that hammocks could be slung at night.

There was no daylight as the portholes were permanently closed to comply with blackout restrictions; in the mornings the atmosphere was foul due to inadequate ventilation.

Few of us had slept in hammocks before. The first night was a shambles as men who had inexpertly slung them climbed in one side and fell out the other. I managed to stay in mine, but regularly cracked my head on the beam as I climbed in. Because of the crowded conditions they were nearly touching, and you were in closer proximity to your neighbour on each side than was ideal.

In the mornings the hammocks had to be taken down and stowed so the mess tables could be used. A few people chose to sleep on deck, but as the weather was cold and wet for most of the voyage I did not consider this to be an acceptable alternative.

The washing and toilet facilities were in the stern and completely inadequate for the number of men on board. There were less than twenty washbasins and a similar number of toilets. The stern suffered the maximum pitching and tossing of the boat, and was the worst place to be for anyone suffering from seasickness.

The toilets consisted of seats fastened over a long metal trough filled with water, which swished backwards and forwards with the movement of the boat. From time to time it was washed away. Later in the voyage the story went round that someone, probably a seaman had lit newspaper and dropped it into the trough. In the few seconds before the flames were extinguished it floated along and scorched one or two bottoms. We were all appalled at this story. Someone said he thought it was arson.

Our ship moved away from the quay soon after we boarded it, and for about twenty-four hours remained anchored in the channel opposite New Brighton. It then set off and we soon joined a convoy, which gradually got bigger as other ships joined it. In total, we had an escort of eight destroyers. I should imagine our route took us well north, because though it was July, the weather remained cold and wet for most of the voyage.

We were very conscious of the danger of U Boats. Fortunately, we were unaware that we were sailing during The Battle Of The Atlantic, when a record number of Allied shipping was sunk. Periodically, men were detailed for submarine spotting; generally the sea was so rough there was little chance of seeing a periscope.

We had Lifeboat Drill from time to time. We donned our life jackets, which we normally used as cushions, and assembled by our allotted lifeboat. It was quite clear there were more men than the lifeboat would take. When we pointed this out to our Sergeant he drew our attention to the loops of rope round the sides to which men could cling if they were unable to get in. We found this far from reassuring, and we did not think there was much chance of getting out of our hold in time if we were torpedoed at night.

A couple of days after we left port, the sea started to get choppy. Sometimes it was very rough indeed, with waves reaching deck height; the ship lurched and shuddered as if it was going to come apart. Early on in the voyage I was seasick and for three or four days I was very miserable. I ate very little and did not wash or shave during this period. I was not alone; there were others in the same condition.

I spent most of my time in some sheltered spot during the day or my hammock in the evening. Most of the time I read a succession of books obtained from a surprisingly good ship's library.

Our food had to be obtained from the ship's galley in the stern, and each mess table provided Mess Orderlies to fetch the food. This meant going to the galley and collecting the food containers, carrying them across quite a long stretch of the open deck and down the stairs to our quarters. Finally, the food was dished out onto individual plates. Not surprisingly, it got cold. The food was not very appetising and fish seemed to be served most days.

Fortunately, I was not an orderly during my seasickness, and had pretty well recovered by the time it was my turn.

An orderly on the next table was not so lucky. Having collected the food, the smell made him nauseous. Nevertheless, he pressed on. When he reached his comrades, a sudden lurch of the ship was his undoing and he was sick over the mess table. This effectively destroyed the appetite of all his mates and a number of onlookers as well.

I got over my seasickness and felt more like mingling with my fellow shipmates. Surprisingly, I bumped into an Airman who used to work in the Frome Co-operative bake house. His trade in the RAF was Cook and Butcher; he became a useful acquaintance when we both ended up in the same RAF camp.

After about eight or nine days, there were signs that we were nearing land. Sea birds were seen and we noticed that our escorting destroyers were starting to leave us.

On our final night at sea I had a personal disaster: my wallet was stolen. We were told to sleep in our clothes in case of an enemy attack at night. We hung our jackets up by our hammocks, giving the culprit access to my wallet. It contained £3.00, all my money, but more important to me also photographs and a keepsake that Eileen had given me when we parted. I was very upset by the loss. When I reported it to the Service Police it was obvious there was no chance of recovering it. The thief would have taken the money, and thrown the wallet and the other contents into the sea.

On the eleventh day, we sailed into Halifax Bay and enjoyed the sight of land after the long days at sea. It was a novelty to see streetlights again after the blackout in Britain. We docked in the early evening, but it was after midnight before we disembarked in full marching order, with our kit.

We marched to a big empty shed where we handed in our gas respirators and the useless topees we had been issued with in West Kirby; some administrative blunder had resulted in them being carried across the Atlantic, and they probably had a return journey.

We were also paid ten dollars, which was comforting for me, as the theft of my wallet had left me penniless. As soon as I could, I invested in a body belt with money pockets. I never again lost money during the whole of my service in the RAF.

Finally, in the early hours of the morning we marched to the railway station and boarded the train that was to take us to our RAF station in Saskatchewan. How surprised we were to be told that even after our sea voyage we were less than halfway to our final destination.

By train across Canada

At the station we were impressed by the size of the train; the engine was huge. Unlike British stations there were no raised platforms, and we boarded the train from ground level with the aid of steps. The coaches were comfortable, with seats that could be converted into beds at night, and with bunks overhead to form additional beds.

What impressed us most was the quality of the food served on the train. There was a cooked breakfast, a substantial lunch at mid-day, and finally a three course dinner in the evening. After the food on the boat this seemed like paradise.

We left Halifax early in the morning; our first stop was at a little town called Truro some three hours later. It was only about 9 o'clock, but to our surprise there was quite a crowd at the station to greet us, and we were given apples by some of the women. What we did not realise at the time was that there had been a great deal of publicity in Canada and the USA about the Battle of Britain, and the RAF were regarded as heroes.

We benefited from this hero worship, not only there, but also at subsequent stops, and indeed for the rest of our stay in Canada. This was very welcome, but quite undeserved, as many of us had not joined the RAF until after the Battle of Britain.

We journeyed on through very picturesque scenery for the rest of the day. The train Conductor, who was the equivalent of the train guard in Britain, said it took about six days to travel right across Canada, and that it was, "Two days of forest, two days of prairie and two days of mountains".

On the second day our principal stop was at Montreal, and we had time to go into the city. I was able to post letters home that I had written in the train. We were surprised to find that in Montreal most of the street signs were in French, and most of the inhabitants spoke it. Here, for the first and only time on our journey, we were pestered by grubby little child beggars asking for pennies.

The only other stop of note that day was at Ottawa, but not for long enough to leave the train. As the Conductor predicted, we travelled through forests for most of the day with little sign of human habitation.

The third day gave us some excitement when we passed an Indian encampment in the woods. We knew all about Red Indians from the many Hollywood western films we had seen, and so were a mite disappointed that on first sight of the train the Indians had not mounted their horses and pursued us, perhaps shooting arrows all the while. As the next stop was called Sioux Lookout, we knew we were indeed in Indian country.

Later in the day, we were told that we would reach Winnipeg at about midnight and would be stopping for just over an hour. Most of us stayed up so that we could see this city.

When we arrived there were people at the station to greet us despite the lateness of the hour. We walked out into the brightly lit streets, and were surprised to find that some shops were still open. I went into an ice-cream parlour and bought ice cream, and then into a drugstore for coffee. We had seen these establishments in Hollywood films, and there we were actually visiting them, and at 1 a.m. in the morning, too. This was really living it up and we thought of poor blacked out Britain.

When we returned to the train we heard that some people had brought cars, and given Airmen a quick tour of the city.

Next morning we woke up to find we were travelling through prairie: flat and uninteresting. According to the Conductor, if we were to go to sleep and wake up twenty-four hours later, looking out of the window we would not know we had moved.

We had a couple of stops at small towns and then early in the afternoon we reached Saskatoon in Saskatchewan. This was quite a large town by Canadian standards, and we stopped long enough to have a quick look at it. I visited it several times during my stay in Canada.

Eventually, at about six o'clock in the evening, and after four days of train travel, we reached our destination: North Battleford, Saskatchewan. We were welcomed in some style by a large crowd, and a brass band playing the National Anthem. Prominent amongst the reception party were two Red Indian chiefs resplendent in their feathered headdresses. We were very impressed, but some weeks later I heard one of the locals refer to an Indian Chief as "Old Jim". This was a complete disillusionment, as I expected them to have much more colourful names — such as Crazy Horse or Lone Eagle, and certainly not Jim.

Lorries soon arrived to take us to the camp, which was about a mile out of town. The camp was newly built and we were the first occupants. The sign outside said it was No. 35 Service Flying Training School, which was always shortened to 35 S.F.T.S.

CHAPTER
SIX

No. 35 S.F.T.S.
RAF North Battleford

Courses at S.F.T.S. were the second stage in the training of pilots. Firstly, they went to an Elementary Flying Training School (E.F.T.S.) where they flew single-engine light aircraft — such as Tiger Moths. Those who passed this course went on to S.F.T.S. where they flew twin-engine aircraft — such as Oxford and Ansons. They also received tuition in a variety of subjects: navigation, bombing, etc. Those who were successful received their "Wings" — the badge worn on their tunic denoting they were pilots. The best Airmen were commissioned to the rank of Pilot Officer, the remainder became Sergeant Pilots.

There were several RAF Flying Training Schools in Canada, mostly in the Prairie Provinces, the building of which commenced early in the war. They had the advantage of good flying conditions, with no danger of enemy attack; a great many RAF pilots were trained by them.

We were well pleased with our accommodation in this new camp. The huts were built in the shape of an "H", with thirty-six double-deck bunks along each of the long sides, and very good ablutions in the short joining piece. We were pleased to be issued with sheets as well as blankets: a luxury unknown in our accommodation in England.

The temperature was in the eighties when we arrived and we were told to change into our khaki drill. This meant wearing shorts so there were many white knees on show.

Next morning, we had our first parade. All except cooks, clerks and equipment assistants were dismissed and had the rest of the day off. This happened on subsequent days, and it soon became clear there was absolutely nothing for the technical trades to do: Flight Mechanics, Armourers, Instrument Mechanics, etc. We had arrived too early: there were no aircraft and no trainee pilots.

This state of affairs continued for about a month. During this time, apart from the occasional drill or PT on the square — and we became skilful at dodging these — we were left to our own devices. We went on parade each morning, were generally dismissed, and then returned to our huts.

The Armourers were all in one hut so we got to know each other. At one of the early parades we were assembled to meet the Flight Sergeant in charge of the Armoury. He admitted he had no work at all for us, as no equipment of any sort had yet arrived.

During these idle days I remember writing letters home; I wrote twice a week to Eileen and almost as frequently to my mother. And also reading for hours on end — there was a very good camp library. There were film shows some evenings, and an occasional concert given by "local talent". We were also allowed out of camp from six o'clock in the evening until midnight.

During this period of inactivity we sometimes had to attend lectures in the Drill Hall. Two of them I still remember.

One, given soon after we arrived, was by a member of the Royal Canadian Mounted Police. We all knew about the Mounties from books and films. They always got their man even if it meant pursuing a wrongdoer for days on end. And so it was with pleasant anticipation that we assembled to hear a representative from this world famous force. His appearance did not disappoint us; he was resplendent in a scarlet jacket and blue trousers, just like we had seen on the films.

Rather disappointingly, the main purpose of his talk was to acquaint us with the complexities of the Saskatchewan licensing laws. We listened in amazement when he told us that alcoholic drinks could be obtained in only two places. There were beer parlours where you could buy beer only, and this had to be drunk while sitting at tables, and not standing at the bar. Ladies were not allowed in; it was an all male preserve. In addition, there were liquor stores where spirits such as whiskey, gin . . . could be bought. However, having bought a bottle of spirits there were strong limitations as to where it could be drunk. Not in the street or the park and certainly not in a beer parlour or a hotel. There seemed no alternative, but to take it home.

75

He then gave us a stern warning about alcohol and the Indians. On no account were we to buy drink for the Indians, even if they bribed us to do so: there had been serious trouble in the past when Indians had become drunk. Some of us nodded wisely when we heard this, because we remembered films where unscrupulous traders had given "fire water" to Indians with disastrous consequences: in no time at all the hero of the film was being tied to a stake and the Indians were lighting a fire under him.

Rather disappointingly he told us no more about Indians, but we all thought it was an interesting, informative talk and right outside our previous experience.

The other lecture was given by a medical officer on the subject of venereal disease. He was a dour Scot, apparently with puritanical convictions, because he delivered his lecture in sombre and forbidding tones and with much emphasis on individual responsibility.

He made it quite clear that he would have little sympathy for anyone stricken by the disease, because it would be their own fault. Then he went on to describe in graphic and dreadful detail exactly what V.D. could do to the male body. At this point two Airmen fainted and had to be taken out.

Completely unmoved, he continued in the same vein to talk about treatment, and before he had finished three more Airmen had to be taken outside to recover.

There was a subdued, but audible speculation in the ranks as to what these five Airmen had been doing since we arrived at North Battleford. As we trooped out after the lecture someone said, "That wasn't much fun was it?"

And that about summed it up.

At about this time the Sergeant in charge of the clothing store (Sgt. Pitts) came to see me. He came from Frome and was a friend of my brother, though I had not previously met him. His wife had written to tell him I was at North Battleford and he had found out from the Orderly Room that I was an Armourer. We exchanged news about Frome then and on later occasions, and despite the difference in our ranks he was always very helpful and friendly. With a Frome man in the cookhouse and another in charge of the clothing store I could look forward to being well fed and clothed during my stay at North Battleford.

Most evenings during this period of inactivity I walked into North Battleford. The weather was good and it was very pleasant to stroll round this little town and have something to eat in one of the cafes, which remained open until quite late. For the first time, I ate hamburgers, and drank ice-cream sodas or iced milkshakes. We knew about these from the Hollywood movies, but, of course, they were not obtainable in Frome. I noted in my diary that I went with a friend to a café and had ham, two eggs, potatoes and peas, followed by apple pie and cream for 45 cents. Then we bought 2 lb of plums, 1 lb of apricots and ½ lb of cherries, and went into the park and ate them. We obviously had good appetites.

I palled up with another Armourer of my age, Peter, who came from Belper in Derbyshire. We did not know it at the time, but we were destined to serve together in various units until almost the end of the war some four years later.

The local people could not have been more friendly or hospitable, they would stop and talk to us and ask us which part of Britain was our home. The children seemed fascinated by us. They had also heard about the Battle of Britain, and in the early days were constantly asking for our autographs.

It seemed to be the custom on fine summer evenings for townspeople to stroll down to the railway station to watch the one train a day going west to arrive, and to see who got off. This gave them the opportunity to meet friends and neighbours, and perhaps have coffee in one of the cafés. Every Sunday evening after the church service there was entertainment of some sort, and coffee and cakes in the church hall; this was a good opportunity to meet local people.

At one of these gatherings I met a family by the name of Tatchell: father, mother and two sons, Lawrence and David, aged fifteen and ten respectively. The father was a Somerset man by birth and had lived near Yeovil before emigrating to Canada in the 1920s. They were extremely kind to Peter and I during our stay in North Battleford, and we were invited to meals countless times.

Mr. Tatchell had a garage business in the town and had a big car, which impressed us very much, so much so I recorded in my diary that it was "over 100 horsepower, does 18 miles to the gallon, and was the same type of car used by the King and Queen when they visited Canada". After supper with the family, he often took us back to camp in this splendid car. And some Sunday afternoons he took us to the lakes, about 30 miles north, for a picnic.

I kept in touch with the Tatchell family long after I left North Battleford. Soon after the war Mrs. Tatchell and Lawrence came to England on a visit to friends and relatives, and spent a day in Frome with Eileen and me. It was an opportunity to thank them again for their kindness during the war years.

Back at camp, despite our idleness we were still being paid, and at my first pay parade I was informed I would get four dollars a week and my mother would get a similar amount. In those days this was the equivalent of about £2 in English money: more than I had been getting in England. I managed reasonably well on this.

When I had been at North Battleford a few weeks I sent a food parcel home to my mother, and in my diary I wrote it contained 2 lb tea, 1½ lb sugar and 1 lb butter, all of which were rationed items in England. This cost $3.50, which I ruefully noted, was almost a week's pay.

Almost a month after our arrival at North Battleford the first batch of pupils arrived. They all had the rank of Leading Aircraftman (LAC) and wore white flashes in their forage caps to denote they were aircrew under training (U/T aircrew). Our first aircraft also arrived; they were mostly twin-engine Oxfords plus one or two

Ansons. At last we started to look like a training camp and our days of idleness were over.

Consignments of small arms, ammunition and pyrotechnics had to be unloaded, recorded and stacked away in the appropriate storehouses; as did machine guns, Browning .303 rifles, revolvers and other armourment equipment to be used for training purposes.

Another chore was the many Air Publications (A.P.s) that arrived with batches of amendments that needed inserting. We spent several days on this boring task.

It became clear that little of what I learned on my Bomb Armourers Course would be of much use here, so I had to buckle down and learn about guns. After a week or two I became proficient at stripping down and re-assembling the Browning machine gun (which was carried on most operational aircraft at that time) and was soon able to instruct pupil pilots.

When night flying started an Armourer was required to be on duty to put reconnaissance flares on the aircraft, and on their return remove any that had not been used and put them back in the armoury store. This meant long boring nights in the flight huts drinking innumerable cups of sweet and well-stewed tea, and talking to other ground crew who were also on duty.

Another task that fell to us Armourers was supervising the firing range when trainees practised machine gun, rifle and pistol firing. Ammunition was issued and usage recorded, and at the end of the session the guns had to be cleaned and put away.

Occasionally the Armourer on duty had the chance to do some firing. I then learnt how difficult it was to hit the target with a pistol shot even at twenty-five yards range. I thought about all the western films I had seen where the hero mounted on a galloping horse drew his pistol and hit an Indian with every shot.

We were also required to operate a Bomb Aiming Simulator where trainees could practise using bombsights. The machinery in this gave me my only war wound: I badly gashed my thumb when incautiously trying to make an adjustment to the machinery without shutting it off.

Perhaps the most boring task of all was duty in the Camera Obscure. This was a windowless building, in the roof of which was a large lens focussed on white paper placed on a table underneath. The roof of the building was painted a bright yellow to make it clearly discernible from the air so that trainees flying over could use it as a target. Photoflashes were fixed to the aircraft, which operated when the bomb aimer's button was pressed.

The resultant flash would be picked up by the lens and showed up on the white paper beneath. By the use of the formula relating to the height and speed of the aircraft etc. it was theoretically possible to say how close to the target a bomb would have landed.

When the aircrew came round to get the result they would shout with disbelief if told they had been way off the target, and would depart muttering that they wished it had been a real bomb so we would know it had been on target.

On hot afternoons it was not easy to stay awake in this dark and stuffy building, and it has to be admitted that it was not uncommon for an Armourer to nod off and miss the flashes. On these occasions he would add one or two crosses to give a reasonably good result with which the aircrew would be happy.

A task that fortunately didn't arise too often was to install a new bombsight in an aircraft and then fly with it to ensure that it was suitable for use. This meant reducing vibrations as much as possible by inserting special washers in the housing. This was not a particularly attractive job as it meant lying on one's stomach in the nose of the aircraft, while the pilot did circuits round the airfield. I used to feel acute nausea for most of the time, so it was not my favourite job and I would avoid it when I could.

After a few weeks a regular routine of work in the armament section was established. The working conditions were generally good and our living conditions were excellent. I was the only Armourer who could type and consequently was given all the clerical and storekeeping work in addition to the day-to-day armament tasks. A series of promotion assessments were carried out and I was soon promoted to AC1 (Aircraftman Grade 1) and a few months later to LAC (Leading Aircraftman). This meant an increase in pay. Most of my colleagues were similarly promoted. LAC was as high as we could go, because the next step to Corporal depended on a vacancy occurring in the fixed quota of NCOs, which seemed rarely to happen.

In charge of the Armament Section was a newly commissioned officer, a humourless and nervous individual who was very anxious not to put a foot wrong. The second in command was a middle-aged Warrant Officer who had been a boy entrant with the RAF and consequently had many years of service. He was a friendly and companionable individual who would frequently entertain us with stories of life in the pre-war RAF. He had little liking for aircrew, probably because they achieved NCO status in months where as it had taken him years.

He would frequently say, "Only birds and bloody fools fly and even the birds don't fly at night," and grumble about the constant talk about flying by aircrew in the Sergeants Mess.

"It's a wonder the men's table don't take off with all that flying talk," he would comment sourly.

We also had a Sergeant and a couple of Corporals who were regulars and had served previously in the RAF. They were amiable and helpful, but slightly contemptuous of us short service wartime recruits.

A regular and rather boring duty was Duty Armourer, which came round about every ten days or so. It meant being on duty in the armoury for twenty-four hours, except for meal breaks, ready to deal with any emergency, which in fact very rarely occurred. Apart from this, we had plenty of free time in the evenings and weekends, and could leave camp as we wished provided we returned by midnight. I used to visit the Tatchell family nearly every week, usually just for coffee and a chat, but sometimes for a meal.

Occasionally they would take us out for the day on a Sunday in their car. Once they took us to visit friends who had a big farm way out in the prairies. We were given lunch and for the first time I ate corn on the cob, which was a delicacy in England at that time. The farms on the prairies had huge acreage compared to British farms, but we were told that the soil was not particularly productive and a large acreage was necessary to make a living.

One day I had a letter from home saying that a friend of my parents knew someone in Saskatoon. Apparently this friend and his wife, a Mr. and Mrs. Hughes, formerly lived in Frome, but had emigrated to Canada in the early 1900s and settled in Saskatoon. They had been in touch recently and the Hughes said they would be delighted to see someone from Frome. Saskatoon was in fact the nearest township of any size, about one hundred miles away and easy to reach by train.

I wrote to them and received a swift reply pressing me to come and see them. I waited until I was due for a forty-eight-hour leave pass, which came up about every couple of months, and set off. On arriving in Saskatoon I booked in for a night at a hotel near the station and went to find their house. They had given me detailed instructions in their letter. I had a terrific welcome and they made a great fuss of me.

Mr. and Mrs. Hughes were in their seventies and living with them was a daughter in her fifties, and three younger women. The latter lodged with the family so they could work in Saskatoon, but their homes were in the country. At our first meeting the Hughes only wanted to talk about Frome and shed a tear or two as they reminisced.

At one point Mr. Hughes left the room and returned bearing a small dried up loaf of bread, which he said he had bought in Frome on the day they had left, some forty years ago, and could never bear to part with it. I visited the family several times whilst I was in Canada and always received a great welcome. Soon after the war one of the women who had lodged with them came to England on a visit and looked us up so we were able to have a brief reunion.

After we had been at North Battleford for a few months a bishop came to officiate at a Sunday service to be held in the Drill Hall. The CO obviously wished to have a good attendance at the service, but as church going was not compulsory he had a quiet word with our Station Warrant Officer (the RAF equivalent of the Army's Sergeant Major) and left the matter in his capable hands.

A parade was ordered for that Sunday morning and we all assembled on the barrack square. The Station Warrant Officer told us that we would be marched to the Drill Hall for the church service, and anyone who did not wish to go was at liberty to fall out. However, he went on to say, in order not to encourage idleness, anyone not going to the service would be given tasks to occupy them for the rest of the morning, which would include scrubbing the cookhouse floor or conveying coal to the boiler house.

Not surprisingly no one objected to going to the service and we all marched off to the Drill Hall.

Probably all would have been well had not the bishop decided to commence his sermon with, what was intended to be, a rhetorical question: "Why are we here?" This was too much for one or two rebellious Airmen who enlightened him in a very positive manner, much to the chagrin of the Station Warrant Officer who with a face like thunder scanned the rear rows of the congregation in the vain hope of spotting the culprits.

Unfortunately, we had one or two fatal crashes whilst I was at North Battleford. These generally occurred when the trainee pilots began flying solo: without an instructor. Sometimes accidents happened when trainees did low flying, often without permission. The authorities realised how hazardous low flying could be when carried out by inexperienced pilots and it was generally banned.

When a fatality occurred the victim was given a military funeral and interred in the local churchyard. One day, I saw on Station Orders that I was included in a list of Airmen detailed for a funeral parade. When I reported for this duty I found there were about twenty in the detail and the Station Warrant Officer picked out half a dozen Airmen of similar height to carry the coffin; and I was one of these selected. We practised for an hour or two, slow marching and carrying a dummy coffin until the SWO was satisfied with our performance.

On the day of the funeral we wore our best uniforms with shiny buttons and well polished boots. We were required to take the coffin from the hearse and carry it to the church. We got the coffin on our shoulders as we had been taught with our arms under it and our hands on the opposite side. We started off and I moved my hand slightly to get a better grip and felt something sticky. Through my mind went all the gruesome stories I had heard about retrieving the mutilated bodies of aircrew from crashed aircraft. I was greatly relieved when we were able to put the coffin down and I discovered that all I had felt was a patch of wet paint.

As mentioned earlier low flying was generally banned except in special circumstances. Low flying without permission was a Court Martial Offence and the penalty was dismissal from flying training and reduction to the ranks. Sometimes pilots just could not resist showing off by low flying over farms or isolated houses and scattering the livestock, generally they would get away with it. The story was told of two senior officers in a train on their return from an RAF station, where they had been attending a Court Martial for a low flying offence. As they journeyed across the prairie, a low flying RAF aircraft travelled alongside; the pilot waggled its wings and waved cheerily. Unfortunately for the Airman, the aircraft number was plainly visible so retribution was inevitable and swift.

The Drill Hall in the camp was marked out as a tennis court with a net that could be put up when the hall was not required for other purposes. Tennis racquets and balls could be borrowed from the equipment store and I used to play quite frequently with my friend Archie. One day there was a notice saying a tennis tournament was to be held and anyone wishing to participate should put their names down; Archie and I both did.

The following week there was another notice listing the competitors for the first round. To my horror I saw that I had been drawn to play the Commanding Officer where as Archie was to play someone equivalent to his own rank. The notice blandly said that competitors should contact their opponents and arrange for matches to be played before the end of the following week. At that time I was an AC1 (Aircraftman First Class), which admittedly was better than AC2, but not much. The Commanding Officer was a Group captain with four gold rings on his tunic and gold braid on his hat and I calculated he was eleven grades higher than me. I couldn't just knock on his door to arrange the match as he was well guarded by secretaries, adjutants and other officers. I had only seen him once and that was when we had a big church parade.

Archie told me not to worry as the Group captain would just tell one of his minions to find out who AC1 Gardner was and I would then receive instructions. However, to be on the safe side I hurried back to my billet, and polished my buttons and boots and pressed my best uniform in case I should be summoned to his presence. My hut mates thought the situation hilarious and dreamed up all sorts of unlikely consequences that could arise from the match: a posting to Iceland was considered the most likely outcome, should I win.

Nothing happened until late afternoon the following day when I was told to report to the Armament Officer. He gave me a puzzled look and said he had received a message from the Group Captain's Office to say that the Commanding Officer wished to play AC1 Gardner at tennis the following afternoon at four o'clock. Not knowing anything about the competition, he was completely mystified to receive such a strange message. I enlightened him how the situation had arisen, and he told me that I had better take the whole of the next afternoon off so as to be sure to be immaculately kitted out, and most importantly to arrive in good time for the match.

The next afternoon, dressed in a clean sports shirt and shorts, and newly whitened shoes, I nervously made my way to the Drill Hall carrying my borrowed racquet and two well-used tennis balls. I was almost half an hour early and passed the time watching two Airmen playing on the court.

At ten to four the Sergeant P.T.I. (Physical Training Instructor) and a Corporal came in. The Sergeant went over and had a word with the Airmen who were playing and they quickly collected up their equipment and scurried off. The Sergeant came over and looked me up and down and confirmed that I was indeed the Group Captain's opponent.

Presently the great man himself came in, greeted me with a cheery smile and suggested we make a start. The Sergeant produced half a dozen brand new tennis balls and the well-worn ones I had brought were contemptuously thrown into a corner. It was now clear

89

that he and the Corporal were to be ball boys. We had the briefest of knock-ups and then tossed for service. I won and elected to serve first. The rules of the tournament said the early rounds would be decided by playing just one set, so I knew it would soon be over.

By the time we started I was very nervous, but to my astonishment my first service was an ace. My opponent never got near it. When returning the ball, the Sergeant gave me a very hard look and I half expected him to say, "Watch it, lad!" But he didn't. In those days I had quite a fast first service, but more often than not it didn't go in. For the rest of the first game I did well and won 40-15. Sadly that was the extent of my triumph.

My opponent won the next game easily; I could do little with his service and in subsequent games he mastered mine; he won the set 6-1. He gave me a warm handshake and disappeared with his retinue of NCOs. But he didn't win the tournament and was knocked out by a fellow officer in the semi-finals. I returned to my billet to announce the result, and my roommates pretended to believe I had deliberately lost to keep in with the authorities.

A few weeks later I was promoted to LAC (Leading Aircraftman) and had to endure a good deal of leg pulling on the lines of "Well, of course, he plays tennis with the Group Captain, so what can you expect?"

CHAPTER
SEVEN

The Canadian Winter

When October arrived, we began to think we would soon start to experience the Canadian winter we had heard so much about from the local people. We had already changed from khaki drill to our familiar and thicker blue uniform. According to local friends, the temperature would be well below freezing for the whole of the winter and on occasions would certainly drop to forty degrees Fahrenheit below zero, which is seventy two degrees of frost. We were also told that in the summer sufficient graves are dug in the churchyard to last until the following spring, as it is impossible to dig them in the winter.

Many houses had unheated cellars that in the winter became the equivalent of the modern freezer and meat etc. could be safely stored in them for weeks in the winter months. All houses had central heating and double-glazing, as did our huts in the camp; heating day and night was essential. Many houses flooded their lawns at the start of the winter and so had their own skating rink. We were to discover that everyone of all ages could skate; small children could soon after they learned to walk.

Before the cold weather started we were all assembled in the Drill Hall to hear a lecture from a medical officer about the dangers of frostbite. It was the same sombre, Scottish medical officer who had given the memorable lecture earlier in the year. He started off in the same uncompromising style by telling us bluntly that we would be given clothing to protect us from frostbite. If we foolishly did not wear it, it would be our own fault if we suffered, and we wouldn't get any sympathy from him. The last remark did not surprise us. He did not strike us as being of a particularly sympathetic nature; and seemed more in the character of an 18th century surgeon who would reprove patients for making a fuss whilst undergoing an amputation without anaesthetic.

He went on to point out that ears were particularly susceptible to frostbite and, when we were outside, we must keep them covered at all times. We had been issued with padded hats with earflaps that could be let down and tied under the chin. We called them "tea cosies" and couldn't imagine wearing them. However, when the cold weather came we soon changed our minds.

The medical officer continued by emphasising the similar need to wear gloves at all times when we were outside, and told us that if we touched a metal object in the open with our bare fingers it might take the skin off in much the same way as a burn.

As a dramatic finale, he explained in graphic detail the likely consequence if anyone was foolish enough to urinate in the open during the cold weather. He then departed leaving us all slightly shaken and a bit apprehensive about the coming months.

In due course winter arrived, the temperature dropped many degrees below freezing and it snowed. The snow was powdery and fine, and didn't thaw at all until the following spring. After one or two days the skies cleared and we had week after week of sunshine followed by more snow and then fine weather again. That seemed to be the pattern: a day or two of snow followed by fine weather, but always very cold.

The temperature did drop to −40°F once or twice, but mostly it was around −20°F, which was bearable unless it was windy, and then it was very unpleasant. Mercifully the extreme temperatures seemed to occur when there was no wind.

At night the spectacular colours of the Aurora Borealis or Northern Lights would illuminate the sky; this occurred so frequently we ceased to comment on it.

Flying continued with relatively few interruptions during the winter and we learnt to cope with the conditions. The Armourers made a sledge to convey flares etc. from the armoury to the aircraft, but it was not much fun dragging this around especially at night.

The only person in the armament section to suffer from frostbite was the Armament Officer. He was perhaps a bit self-conscious about walking outside with his earflaps down and tied under his chin. His ears were quite badly frostbitten and became very swollen, and then drooped a bit like a cocker spaniel. There was speculation amongst the Armourers as to whether they would fall off or not: the Medical Officer's talk was still fresh in mind. Happily they didn't, but he must have had a painful couple of weeks and probably received scant sympathy when he visited Sickbay.

If bad weather — snowstorms or fog — were forecast by the Met. Office, flying was cancelled. But there was always the possibility of sudden fog or snow arriving when aircraft were away on a long cross-country flight, and on their return they might have difficulty locating the airfield. There were some runway lights and, as there was no blackout, the lights from the hangers and other buildings helped. In addition the Armourers had two devises to indicate the location of the airfield: one was a large rocket described in RAF parlance as "Rockets, signal, ½ lb," and the other was a signal mortar: "Mortars, signal 3". The rocket would rise to a height of just over 1,000 feet and then emit two-dozen stars, and the mortar would propel a large flare to about the same height. We had all learned about them in armament school, but had not actually fired them; so our armament officer decided that as winter was approaching a practise should be carried out.

One morning half a dozen of us assembled near the control tower and it was decided that we would start off by firing a couple of rockets. A tripod was provided (Tripod, rocket, signal) into which the rocket was placed and this elevated it to a near vertical position. The NCO in charge, after prudently checking to see no aircraft was overhead, told an Armourer to light the rocket. Our activity had attracted the attention of some of the control tower staff and one or two passing Airmen, so we had some spectators. The rocket was lit using another pyrotechnic called a port fire which, when lit, emitted a flame a couple of inches long, which was then applied to the base of the rocket. The Armourer, never having done this before, was a little nervous and when smoke and flames started to come from the rocket he backed away hurriedly; and in his haste knocked over the tripod. Consequently, instead of rising into the air it shot off across the airfield about a foot above ground level, very narrowly missing an aircraft and several Airmen who were working on it. The rocket continued its progress across the airfield fortunately not hitting anything until it was halted by the perimeter fence, when it dutifully emitted its two dozen stars and died.

After a moment's stunned silence there were howls of indignation and rage from the Airmen who'd had such a narrow escape. They came stamping over to demand an explanation. One claimed the rocket had passed between his legs, which was surely a gross exaggeration. But he had to be believed when he shouted, "It sure as hell scared the living daylights out of me!"

Our shamefaced explanation, "Well, you see, the tripod fell over," seemed a little inadequate.

Eventually they stumped off crossly muttering, "Bloody Armourers will kill someone before they've finished."

As an officer in the watchtower had observed the incident there had to be an enquiry. After reprimands all round one useful outcome was that a method was found of securely anchoring the tripod to the ground so that it couldn't be knocked over by clumsy Airmen.

A few days later we returned to fire the signal mortar. The rocket incident was still fresh in mind and our activities were watched with interest by staff in the watchtower; and there was some jeering from Airmen on the airfield. The mortar consisted of a steel tube about 3 inches in diameter, which was the barrel, and this was inserted into a base that had been firmly bolted to the ground. The method of operation was quite simple, indeed rather primitive. A bag of gunpowder was dropped down the barrel followed by the flare, which was in a cardboard cylinder about the size of a cocoa tin.

At the base of the barrel was a small tube, which was the igniter. A lanyard was attached to this tube. The Armourer retreated a few yards and pulled on the lanyard. This caused the igniter to fire a flame into the gunpowder, which exploded and lit the flare and sent it about 1,000 feet into the air. This time everything worked perfectly. The mortar produced a satisfying loud explosion that rattled all the windows in the watchtower and the flare rose perfectly in the air. There was some jeering from the Airmen who shouted, "You missed us, you missed us!" But it was a very acceptable exercise, and to make sure we fired two more.

Whilst carrying out this exercise we all remembered being told at the Armament School that after the first round had been fired smouldering fragments from the bag of gunpowder could be left in the base of the barrel and prematurely ignite the next round. I remember the instructor's explicit warning: "Don't ever look down the barrel or it might be your silly head that goes up 1,000 feet in the air."

We did use both rockets and the mortars once or twice during the winter when fog had suddenly descended on the airfield. On one occasion when I was Duty Armourer I was called out to fire the mortar. I took the necessary equipment with me — flares and gunpowder — but when I removed the cover from the mortar I found to my horror that the barrel was half full of snow. I scooped out as much as I could, then to a background of shouts of "Hurry up" from the watchtower I quickly dropped both gunpowder and flare down the barrel and hurriedly pulled the lanyard. My worry was that the gunpowder might be made too damp to ignite at all or delay firing until an aircraft, which was rapidly approaching, was directly overhead. I dreaded to think what would be the penalty for hitting and perhaps destroying an aircraft.

Mercifully, all went well and the flare rose in the air at just the right time, and in addition there was a most impressive smoke ring perhaps due to the damp gunpowder. I fired two more rounds and the aircraft eventually landed safely, but I have no idea how much of a help the signal mortar was.

The end of the year approached and I duly experienced the novelty of an RAF Christmas Dinner when the

NCOs and officers waited on the Airmen. A very good dinner it was, too, as one might expect in non-rationed Canada. And we were also each given a mug full of beer.

I looked back on what was a very momentous year for me. I had been taken into the RAF from a rural backwater in Frome and very quickly transported across the Atlantic to Canada and, as we learned later, at the height of the U-boat campaign. Then the train took us halfway across the continent to a spot in the heart of Saskatchewan, an area that had never featured in my geography lessons at school.

My RAF training in England had been sketchy to say the least: I had been given six weeks training on bombs and then posted to an RAF station that didn't have them and where Armourers mostly worked on guns. I, therefore, had to learn as I went along. I was conscious of my good fortune in being in a safe area where food was plentiful and living conditions good.

We learned much later that we were extremely lucky as the other draft at West Kirby at that time went to Singapore, and arrived only a few weeks before the Japanese attack. Many of those Airmen would have been taken prisoner or killed. It was pure chance as to which of the two drafts an individual was allotted.

CHAPTER
EIGHT

1942

The first few months of 1942 passed uneventfully at North Battleford. We felt more optimistic about the outcome of the war now that the USA had been brought in, following the attack on Pearl Harbour, even though the news continued to be gloomy, because of the initial Japanese successes in the Far East. However, in our remote backwater at North Battleford far away from military activity the daily routine continued uneventfully.

Our armament duties were not too demanding. At the Firing Range, we supervised the firing of the Browning machine gun and various small arms, such as revolvers. Afterwards we stripped and cleaned the guns. We took it in turns to be in the Bombing Instructor or the Camera Obscurer, and sometimes we were in the classroom showing trainees how to strip and assemble the machine guns. In addition I carried out some office duties and was responsible for keeping the records of ammunition and pyrotechnics up to date.

Night duties came round about once a week, when we had to fit reconnaissance flares to aircraft for use in an emergency, and remove any that had not been used on the aircraft's return. We had got used to working in the very cold weather and made sure we didn't get frostbite.

Sundays were normally free, and often friends in North Battleford invited me to lunch. Some evenings we watched a film in the camp gym; there were no chairs so we brought our pillows and sat on the floor.

There was also a camp concert, and a band that entertained us from time to time. At least once a week, and sometimes more often, I played tennis in the Drill Hall with my friend Archie. I had always regarded tennis as purely a summer game, and it seemed odd to be walking through all the snow on my way to the Drill Hall carrying my tennis equipment.

Since I had been at North Battleford I had been promoted twice — AC2 to AC1, and AC1 to LAC — but had never received any additional pay. My frequent enquiries at the Pay Office were met by the response that my records had not been received from England and, therefore, I could only be paid at the basic rate. Why this should be I was never able to find out. However at the end of April I received the good news that my records had arrived and I would receive all my back pay at the next payday.

With the prospect of so much wealth I thought about a holiday, particularly as I found I could have two weeks' leave, my entitlement for the year. My plan was to go by train through the Rockies to Vancouver, have a few days there, and return by the same route, perhaps stopping off in the Rockies for a day or two en route. I thought the journey would be a little under a thousand miles each way.

I asked my friend Archie if he would like to join me on this trip; though he was very willing he did not have enough money. I calculated my back pay would be sufficient for both of us, so I offered to lend him half and he undertook to pay me back by instalments on our return; this he dutifully did over the course of a few weeks. We made our plans, obtained our leave passes and arranged to depart on the evening of payday.

The big day, May 15th eventually arrived and I eagerly attended the pay parade. The procedure was for us to assemble in the Drill Hall. A table would be set up in the front at which sat the Pay Officer and a Sergeant. The latter would call out the names in alphabetical order and the amount to be paid. The Airman named would march out to the table, salute and receive the money from the officer. The named amount for an Airman would be from ten to fifteen dollars, but when the Sergeant came to my name he announced, "One hundred and thirty dollars". There was an audible gasp from the assembled Airmen and much craning of necks to see the lucky Airman. The Pay Officer did a palpable double take and was deep in conversation with the Sergeant when I marched up to the table. Reassurance was obviously forthcoming, and the full amount paid out.

I met Archie after the Pay Parade and handed over half my new wealth, and that afternoon prepared for our trip to Vancouver. So it was that at about 10p.m. on May 15th we left North Battleford on the one train a day that went west, and travelled through the night across the prairies to Edmonton, which we reached at about 7 a.m. the next morning. We had to change from Canadian National that had brought us from North Battleford, to Canadian Pacific, which was to take us on to Vancouver.

The two train companies worked quite independently of each other, and used separate stations and even separate rail tracks, which seemed to us rather wasteful in view of the huge distances covered. The railway stations had no platforms, the train staff brought out steps to enable passengers to board the train.

After a quick breakfast at the station we caught the 8 a.m. train to Calgary. Once again, we travelled through prairie and passed through small towns and villages; one was called Red Deer, which we thought was a very appropriate name for a frontier type town. At about mid-day, we caught our first glimpse of the snow-covered peaks of the Rockies far away in the distance. An exciting moment.

We arrived in Calgary early in the afternoon to find quite a big city, population at that time was about 90,000. Accommodation was not difficult to find and we were able to book a twin bedded room in quite a good class hotel for two dollars, giving us confidence that our one hundred and thirty dollars would last out.

Later, we went for a stroll and found the National History Park in which were life size replicas of pre-historic animals, dinosaurs ... we were very impressed. That evening after supper we explored the city marvelling at the many lights and the high-rise buildings; such a contrast to blacked out Britain. One had fourteen stories. We had never seen anything like it!

The Hudson Bay Company had a huge store and the name conjured up visions of fur trappers and traders in the frozen north.

After breakfast we caught the next train going west and within a couple of hours were travelling between great white peaks and the scenery was everything we had expected. We arrived at Banff at lunchtime and broke our journey there, intending to travel on to Vancouver the next day. Banff was a small town, with a population of about 2,500 at that time, completely surrounded by huge snow capped mountains, some as high as 10,000 feet.

Again, we found accommodation in a cheap hotel, just 50 cents a night — about three shillings in English money at that time. My room was about 9ft × 4ft, not really room to swing even a small cat, but it had glorious views from the window, and the price gave us even greater confidence in our ability to manage our finances.

While we were in Banff we walked along the River Bow and marvelled at the spectacular scenery all around. We also saw a fish hatchery where they raised rainbow trout from spawn to huge fish, something quite new to us. About two miles out was the Banff National Park, where we saw buffalo and moose. And in the distance, was the Banff Springs Hotel, a very up market establishment where royalty and other nobility stayed, and far out of reach of a couple of Airmen on a tight budget.

The next morning we caught the mid-day train to Vancouver and again journeyed through the most fantastic mountain scenery. We stopped briefly at a spot, called the Great Divide, where a stream forked; it was claimed that the water from one branch eventually reached the Pacific and the other the Atlantic.

Then on we travelled, to the beautiful Yoho Valley. In the notes I made at the time I described it as "Awe inspiring and indescribably beautiful". On we went along the Kicking Horse Canyon, ". . . where the rushing swirling river raced between sheer mountain walls." And then, "The breath taking 150 feet fissure in solid rock . . . the Albert Canyon." I think some of these descriptions were taken from the guidebook. At dusk we reached the lovely Lake Shuswap and were able to admire the reflection of the setting sun as it went down behind the mountains. When night came we were not able to see the scenery through which we passed, and so we settled down to sleep.

We awoke quite early and were able to see the final spectacular view called Hellgate, where the river rushes through a steep canyon. After that the scenery was more like England, with slow moving rivers and green fields, but still a contrast to the drab prairies around North Battleford.

We arrived in Vancouver at about 9.30 and it was raining — again, rather like England. We went to a café for breakfast during which we discovered that the RAF was still a novelty in Vancouver. On hearing us talk the waitress said, "Gee, are you from England?"

When we admitted it — though in fact Archie came from Scotland, but we didn't want to complicate matters — she went and told the proprietor. He came over and made a point of shaking hands with us, and wishing us well. He said the meal was on the house and declared rather dramatically "No RAF boy pays for a meal in my restaurant!" This was good news, and we felt even more confident about our holiday money lasting out. No doubt later in the war when RAF uniforms became rather more common in Vancouver, the proprietor would become rather less accommodating.

Other customers in the restaurant, on hearing what was said, came over and wished us well. We tried to look suitably heroic as we ploughed through our free meal of two eggs, bacon, sausage, beans, mushrooms and fried bread. The Battle of Britain had received so much publicity in Canada that RAF Airmen were regarded as heroes. How could we tell them that we hadn't joined the RAF until the Battle of Britain was over?

Having escaped from our well-wishers we looked for somewhere to stay and booked into a hotel in the centre of the city. Sadly there were no special terms or discounts for RAF heroes, so we concluded that the proprietor had German origins.

Later in the day we started to explore the city and soon found the Service Enquiry Institute we had heard about from a previous visitor to Vancouver. This was a splendid establishment that not only provided cups of tea for servicemen, but also maintained a long list of addresses of residents who had formerly lived in the United Kingdom and now wished to provide accommodation for British servicemen.

Against each name was the area in the UK from which they originated. Somerset was not mentioned so we thought we would try someone from Scotland for the benefit of Archie who hailed from Oban.

The good lady was phoned and apparently said that she would be delighted to accommodate us and would we come along about mid-day the following day. That having been settled we set off to do more sight seeing, but the weather was so wet we went to the cinema in the afternoon and again in the evening. After a late supper in a Chinese Restaurant, where obviously they knew nothing about the gallant RAF and we had to pay, we returned to our hotel.

Next morning we set off for the address we had been given: a twenty-minute ride by bus and then a short walk. We were welcomed by our hostess and her two children and given lunch. They were extremely hospitable and after we had eaten we were shown to two very nice bedrooms; it was clear that we would be very comfortable here. At her suggestion we spent the afternoon at Stanley Park, the principal park of the city and some two miles across. It was well laid out and had great views across the bay.

One unwelcome reminder of the war was the sight of two Blenheim aircraft carrying out practice bombing over the bay. We were also told there was to be a practice blackout in the city that night. Canada's West Coast was within the range of the Japanese Navy and I believe that later that year a submarine actually fired a few shells at the city.

We had supper in town and returned to our "billet" in time to avoid the blackout, and were introduced to our host who had been at work when we arrived. We stayed up very late talking to our host and hostess who were very eager to hear anything we could tell them about the "old country" from which they had emigrated some twenty years before.

The following week was idyllic. The weather was good almost all of the time, our accommodation was superb and we had an interesting and beautiful city to explore. We had a cooked breakfast every morning and ate out the rest of the day returning late evening to relate our "adventures".

One day we took a ferry to North Vancouver to visit Capilano, another beauty spot. The main feature was Capilano Canyon across which a narrow bridge was secured by two steel cables; it swayed slightly when walked upon, but gave a good view of the river some 200 ft below. We hesitated slightly when we approached this structure, but other people were going across and we thought it wouldn't do for "heroic RAF Airmen" to be seen hanging back. With some misgivings we crossed the bridge and were mightily relieved to reach the other side, only to discover that we had to make a return journey, as there was no other way out.

We spent the rest of the afternoon descending numerous steps to the foot of the canyon. When we looked up at the bridge, which seemed very flimsy from this angle, we were very glad we did not have to cross it again.

Another day when we were walking in a park we passed a large internment camp for Japanese civilians, men, women and children. Apparently after Pearl Harbour all Japanese citizens in the city and surrounding area were rounded up, and I believe they remained so until after the war. This resulted in the closure of a good many small businesses in the city.

We thought our trip to the west coast of Canada wouldn't be complete without a visit to Vancouver Island, so we set off early one morning to catch the boat to Victoria, the capital of the island. We were a little surprised to find the journey would take five hours. I suppose we thought it would be like going to the Isle of Wight from Portsmouth. However, it was a most delightful trip, we were sailing between the mainland and a number of little islands covered with thick vegetation down to the water's edge. We were never out of sight of land and the sea was very calm.

On arriving at Victoria we found we would not have much time for sightseeing, because in order to catch a return boat, to get us back that night, we had to make a three hour journey by bus across the island to the small town of Nanimo. In the couple of hours or so we had in Victoria we did some sightseeing, admired the splendid Government buildings and also observed that the police wore British style police uniforms complete with helmets. It seemed to have a high proportion of retired people, many of them British, and it reminded me a little of Bath. Then we had our three-hour bus ride to the pretty little town of Nanimo and were able to see more of Vancouver Island from the bus window. We arrived in time to catch the boat and found we had a little shorter voyage of about three hours, and we landed at midnight. There were plenty of restaurants still open so we were able to have a very late supper before returning to our billet in the small hours.

Our holiday in Vancouver was drawing to a close. We had done a good deal of memorable sightseeing and also spent some pleasurable hours laying in the sun and reading. On our last day we got up late and had a combined breakfast and lunch before doing a tour of the shops including an enormous Hudson Bay Company store. We bought presents for the family that had looked after us so well, and that evening we took them all out to the cinema. Nevertheless, we still stayed up for a final late night chat, which had been our routine almost every evening of our stay.

Next morning we regretfully said our goodbyes and made our way to the station. We were sad to be leaving; it had been such a memorable week for us. Not only had we seen so much wonderful scenery, but also everywhere the people of Vancouver had treated us with great kindness. But we could not stay longer; it was time to start the long journey back to North Battleford.

At ten o'clock that morning we were on a train heading for Calgary. We passed through magnificent scenery along the Fraser Valley, but later in the day it started to rain and when we reached Syracuse Lake, an acclaimed beauty spot, the mist and rain almost hid it from view.

We slept in the train and early next morning we stopped at the town of Golden. It had been our intention to break our journey here, to see the famed Lake Louise, but as it was pouring with rain we decided to stay on the train and go on to Calgary. Despite the rain we were able to appreciate the beauty of the Yoho Valley and the grandeur of the snow capped mountains around Banff.

We arrived at Calgary at lunchtime and booked in at the same hotel we had used on our outward journey. As it was still wet we were reduced to filling in the time by going to the cinema in the afternoon, having tea and then going to a different cinema in the evening. After supper we walked the short distance to our hotel, it was snowing even though it was the end of May.

Next morning we resumed our journey by catching a train to Edmonton. It was still snowing when we left Calgary, but it was fine by the time we arrived mid afternoon. We had a meal and did a little sightseeing, mainly Government Buildings and large stores including the ubiquitous Hudson Bay Company.

We eventually gave up and sought refuge in a cinema emerging in time to have supper and catch the 10.30p.m. train to North Battleford. Soon after eight the next morning we arrived and our holiday was over.

Our first port of call was to a local restaurant where we had a very large breakfast whilst we discussed our holiday. Our funds had lasted very well and we still had some of our $130 left. This was primarily due to the fact that, though we had been away for fifteen nights, we had only had to pay for hotel accommodation for four nights, and even then we had chosen cheap hotels. While in Vancouver we had free accommodation for seven nights and then on the outward and return journeys we had slept in the train two nights each way at no extra cost.

Altogether we considered that our holiday had been a great success and rather sadly we returned to reality by catching a train back to camp.

CHAPTER
NINE

Return to North Battleford

There was sad news for Archie when he returned: a letter from his parents telling him that his brother, an RAF Air Gunner, had not returned from a bombing mission over Germany and was, therefore, reported missing. We tried to be as optimistic as possible saying that he would turn up eventually as a prisoner of war. However, as we feared, it was confirmed a few weeks later that he had been killed.

It was back to the usual routine and the holiday began to fade from memory. Soon after our return there was a station order saying that we would change from our blue uniform to khaki drill on June 1st. The weather had turned a little chilly during the last few days so none of us were very enthusiastic about donning shorts. However the order made no concession to the temperature so khaki drill it had to be. We were told to parade at 8a.m. so the Station Warrant Officer (SWO) could carry out an inspection.

We duly assembled that morning, and I noticed that one Airman was wearing his winter issue "Long John" combinations under his shorts, which did a splendid job of keeping his knees warm. He argued that the order said nothing about underwear and he thought he could be forgiven for wearing something warm under the regulation shorts. I thought he was unduly optimistic if he thought the SWO would see it his way.

I knew the SWO was a fierce disciplinarian and not best known for a forgiving nature or a sense of humour. I positioned myself in the parade where I had a clear view of what I thought would be an interesting confrontation. The SWO strode along the ranks casting a baleful eye over the assembled Airmen, then stopped abruptly when he caught sight of the combinations.

He seemed momentarily stunned and the Airman made use of the slight pause to politely make the point that the order made no mention of underwear. The SWO gave him little time to explain before thrusting his face close to the Airman and announcing, in tones that could be heard right across the camp, that he had no time for smart-Alec comedians. He then went on to say he could do something about the Airman's cold knees and summonsed a Sergeant and instructed him to see that the Airman ran three times round the barrack square before returning to the hut to get properly dressed.

The inspection was completed and as we marched off we saw the unfortunate Airman wearily pounding his way around the square. He certainly didn't look cold any more.

One weekend towards the end of summer, there was a carnival in town complete with a procession that included floats and local bands. On one of the floats were a number of elderly Indians who were said to be the remaining survivors of the Louis Riel Rebellion. This took place in Saskatchewan towards the end of the 19th century and was led by Louis Riel, a Canadian half-caste. There was some loss of life, but the rebellion was suppressed by the Mounties, no doubt with military support.

The elderly Indian gentlemen on the float looked harmless enough; it was, no doubt, very different some fifty years before when outlying farms were attacked. A good many Indians came into town for the carnival, more than we had seen before. They were from a reservation a few miles away, and brought horses to sell at the fairground. Their women folk wearing brightly coloured clothes could be seen in the town.

Farewell to North Battleford

The summer passed uneventfully until, in September, I received the staggering news that I was to be posted away from North Battleford to an RAF station at Weyburn: about three hundred miles to the south and not far from the border with the USA. There were a number of postings away at this time; the reason being that most of the Airmen at North Battleford had arrived together when the camp was opened in July 1941, and would be due to return to the UK when their two year tour was completed in the summer of 1943. It was necessary to have a change over of staff well before that date so North Battleford would not lose its entire experienced staff at the same time.

I was sad to leave. I had enjoyed my stay there and made many friends. It was there that I learned about life in Canada and how it differed from England. I had learned to cope with the extreme weather, cold almost beyond belief in the winter and very hot in summer.

North Battleford was a small town, much smaller than my hometown Frome, yet it had several restaurants that were open for breakfast and stayed open until late at night. This would be unthinkable in small towns in England. Meals were cheap and well within the means of not particularly affluent Airmen; we had got into the habit of eating out in the evenings quite frequently. We had become used to what seemed to us strange licensing laws, and, though we missed the English pubs, there were many compensations.

I was sorry to part with the civilian friends I had made at North Battleford. The local residents were very good to us and, as I mentioned earlier, one family in particular, the Tatchells, treated me almost as family. And I knew I would miss very much their welcoming home that I visited so often.

Also, I had made several good friends amongst my fellow Airmen and one that I valued highly was Jack. He was an Armourer, too, a Londoner, married and ten years older than me. Whilst I was a country boy who had never been far from home, he was a sophisticated city dweller who had worked for several years as a salesman, and was eloquent and full of confidence. He took me under his wing to some extent. We had some good times together and he taught me a great deal, probably more than he realised. His great good humour even during difficult times was an inspiration. Although we didn't know it, when we said goodbye at North Battleford we were to meet up again the following year when we returned to England, and were then destined to serve again at various RAF stations until the end of the war.

Another good friend was Archie who accompanied me on our trip to Vancouver. He was a Scot from Oban, fresh out of university and very much an intellectual. We used to have long discussions on varied subjects ranging from politics to art and literature, from which I learned much. After I left North Battleford we didn't see each other or correspond until surprisingly forty years later when he wrote to me, by which time we had both retired.

When going through some old papers he found my address in Frome and sent me a letter. By this time the house in which I used to live had been pulled down, but the postman knew my brother and passed the letter to him and so it reached me.

I saw that Archie was now living in Sunderland and, quite by chance, Eileen and I had planned a holiday in North Yorkshire that summer, so we arranged to call on him. Archie and his wife received us kindly and gave us a good lunch, but it was a sad meeting in many ways. He was in poor health and obviously living in straitened circumstances in a run down part of Sunderland, which showed clear evidence of vandalism. Although we

116

reminisced, the magic of our youthful companionship could not be recaptured; it belonged to a past age. Also after forty years of completely different lifestyles we had little in common. We parted knowing we would never see each other again. I sent a "thank-you" letter on our return home, but never heard further from him.

One other friend at North Battleford who provided much stimulated conversation was Colin, a fellow Armourer. He was from Glasgow and had been brought up in the Gorbals, and, perhaps not surprisingly, was a communist. His background and upbringing was way outside my experience and I learned much from him. He persuaded me to read Marx, which I found much too hard going, and "No Mean City", which I enjoyed.

In return I told him about life in rural Somerset and what it was like working for a great landowner, the Marquis of Bath. Colin seemed fascinated by my stories, but would often shake his head sadly and say, "Come the revolution!" After leaving North Battleford I never saw him again, but heard that after the war he emigrated to Canada.

Although they were not friends, there were two characters at North Battleford who I still remember. One was Jimmy Edwards who after the war became a well-known comedian on stage, radio and television. He was a Trainee Pilot, accomplished enough to receive a commission at the end of the course, and went on to serve with distinction in the RAF for the rest of the war. Whilst at North Battleford, he was a prominent member of the station concert party, and also played in the station dance band.

The other person was an Airman who prior to the war was classed as The Yo-Yo Champion Of The World, and appeared as such in The Guinness Book of Records. He would sometimes display his skills at camp concerts.

Eventually the date for my departure from North Battleford arrived. And after saying my goodbyes I carried my kit bag to the guardroom and was then taken by lorry to the railway station. No other Airmen were going so I travelled on my own. First, I took the train to Saskatoon and from there travelled some two hundred miles south to Regina: the nearest town of any size to my new base.

41 SFTS Weyburn

I had to wait for a local train to take me a further fifty miles or so to Weyburn. A lorry met the train to convey me to my new home at 41 SFTS Weyburn.

The layout of the camp was very similar to North Battleford, the principal difference being the type of aircraft. Instead of the dual engine Oxford and Anson used at North Battleford we had the single engine Harvard. The Trainees at Weyburn were likely to eventually go to Fighter Command, whereas North Battleford Trainees were destined for Bomber or Coastal Command.

The Harvard was a very noisy aircraft and when directly overhead made an ear piercing sound. My first thought was that I would never get to sleep when night flying was in process, but I soon got used to it and like everyone else slept perfectly. The surrounding area was very like that at North Battleford, miles and miles of prairie stretching right down to the USA border, about fifty miles away, and probably beyond.

The little town of Weyburn, similar in size to North Battleford, was within walking distance of the camp.

On my first day I followed the usual procedure of taking an Arrival Form round the various sections to be checked in. On going to the Admin. Section I discovered that the Squadron Leader in charge was formerly the bank manager in Frome. His son had been a school friend of mine, and was now in the RAF; we corresponded from time to time.

I went in to see him and we chatted for a while about his son and prewar Frome. I eventually took my leave, but we never met again, the disparity in our ranks was too great for any social meetings.

I soon settled into my new surroundings, my fellow Armourers were a convivial crowd and easy to get on with. I did have a surprise when I met the Armourment Officer. He had formerly been a Flight Sergeant at North Battleford, and had been commissioned and posted to Weyburn. The work was similar to that at North Battleford, the main difference was that we fitted Camera Guns to the aircraft to record the pilot's success, or lack of it, when carrying out mock attacks

119

on targets. There was some night work that involved fitting flares etc. to the aircraft, and this came round about once a week.

Two new arrivals from England gave us some amusement when they moved into our hut. They seemed convinced they were in the Wild West they had seen in so many Hollywood films, particularly as they had glimpsed one or two Indian reservations on their journey across Saskatchewan. They had even bought cowboy hats in a local store to take home as souvenirs.

When they discovered that there were stables nearby where horses could be hired by the hour, they were determined to have a go at riding; perhaps thinking they might be able to emulate their film star heroes. One afternoon they set off for their first ride and we hoped they would return undamaged.

Later that day, just one returned and recounted his sad story. Apparently, they did not tell the stable owner that their only experience of riding had been on seaside donkeys. They were mounted on a couple of stable horses and sent on their way. They set off at a gentle trot, but after about a quarter of an hour they were feeling confident and wanted something more exciting. They decided to have a race, such as they had seen on cowboy films, so they dug in their heels and let out the sort of piercing yells that they had heard film cowboys make.

The startled animals took off at full speed, much faster than the Airmen had anticipated, and they had no idea how to make the horses slow down. They were in grave danger of being thrown off, and were reduced to clinging to the mane and shouting every command for stop they knew.

Eventually the storyteller's horse slowed down and he was able to scramble off, but his companion's was still going flat out and disappeared into the distance. There were no hedges or fences to bar its way. Once he had got his feet on the ground nothing would have persuaded our Airman to get back on, so rather ignominiously he walked back to the stable leading the horse. When the stable man enquired about his mate he could only point at the horizon saying, "He was going in that direction when I last saw him."

After hearing his story, we speculated on the likely fate of the missing Airman if he reached the USA border wearing RAF uniform and a cowboy hat. Much later that evening he returned, very saddle sore after his ordeal. He did not reach the USA border, but went a long way and had to be rescued by one of the stable hands who rode out to find him, and for which service he had to pay.

The remaining months of 1942 passed uneventfully. The work had become routine: gun cleaning, fitting equipment to aircraft, attendance at the gun range . . . Time off was spent either reading — there was a good camp library — or playing snooker in the NAAFI with fellow Armourers. Occasionally we went to Weyburn for shopping or to have a meal in one of the restaurants.

I had one weekend pass, which enabled me to visit Regina, stay in a hotel and do some sightseeing. There was not all that much to see apart from the usual Government Buildings and the headquarters of the Royal Canadian Mounted Police. There were a number of big stores including the inevitable Hudson Bay Company.

Christmas arrived and we had the traditional Christmas dinner served to the Airmen by Officers and NCOs. This was very good, but brought back memories of past Christmases at home.

Directly after Christmas I had a few days leave, which I spent at Saskatoon. It was a longer journey than from North Battleford. I was able to catch an evening train from Weyburn to Regina, stay there overnight and continue on to Saskatoon in the morning. I stayed at a hotel in Saskatoon and was able to renew acquaintance with the family I used to visit from North Battleford — the mother and father originally lived in Frome.

I spent every evening with them and we either ate in or went to a restaurant. One evening, I went to an ice-hockey match for the first time. I was impressed by the speed of play, but was soon aware of how cold it was for spectators and was grateful for the hot drink available at the interval.

Whilst there I celebrated my 21st birthday. The family laid on a special meal and a party for me, and it was a great climax to what had been an eventful year. I knew I was to return to the UK in 1943 so I could not fail to wonder where I would be on my next birthday. I noted in my diary that the temperature on my birthday was forty-five degrees below zero Fahrenheit.

CHAPTER
TEN

1943

The weather was a little milder at the start of the New Year and there was even a partial thaw one day. When it froze at night the roads were like glass, and everyone was slipping and sliding on the icy surfaces.

Within a few days we felt the full impact of a Canadian winter; the temperature dropped to forty degrees below zero Fahrenheit and there was a heavy snowfall. All flying had to be abandoned even though snowploughs worked day and night to clear the runways. There was a foot of snow and the wind caused drifts up to five feet; some parked vehicles were almost completely covered.

We were issued with fleecy lined moccasin boots, which were ideal for these temperatures. After a few days it was possible to resume flying day and night, but working outside in the intense cold was dreadful. We used sledges to carry equipment out to the aircraft and we were encased in thick clothing from head to foot. We wore woollen gloves and over them thick mittens.

We remembered the MO's warning about touching metal with bare hands, "The skin will be taken off the hand similar to a burn." One or two blizzards sprang up quickly while aircraft were flying and the Armourers were called out to fire the signal mortar to help them land. Fortunately there were no crashes.

For a couple of days early in February I felt a little off colour and had a sore throat. Then one morning, one of the chaps said, "You've got spots!" and hastily backed away.

My other roommates approached, but not too closely, and confirmed, "He's right! You're covered!" There was some speculation as to the cause, ranging from all the better-known diseases to some made up ones. They were unanimous in their opinion that it was certainly infectious, and that I should remove my infected person from the room immediately and depart to the Station Sick Quarters, also advising me to take my washing and shaving things, as I would probably be there a long time, and not to send them any notes on infected writing paper.

With these less than comforting words in my ears I made my way to the Sick Quarters where the Medical Officer promptly diagnosed, "Measles!" and ordered me to an isolation ward.

I was unwell for two or three days. After that I felt fine, but was still made to stay in bed for a week. Then I was allowed up in the daytime and joined other measles patients in a convalescent ward. We whiled away the time by talking, reading, listening to the radio and playing cards. It was at this time that I learned to play bridge. It was really very comfortable; we were warm and well fed, and able to look through our double glazed windows at the snow and ice outside.

I learned that my roommates had been confined to camp and had to report periodically to the Sick Quarters to be checked. One morning, I saw them trudging through the snow and cheerfully waved to them from the window. They responded grumpily by shaking their fists.

After I had been in hospital a fortnight and was due to be released, one of our patients developed scarlet fever and was quickly transferred to the scarlet fever ward. The medical officer was furious when he heard of this cross infection and we measles patients had to have another week in our ward to ensure that we hadn't been infected. We were not displeased to have an extension to our stay in these comfortable surroundings, and were even more pleased when we heard we were entitled to sick leave when finally discharged.

Eventually, after a stay in hospital of more than three weeks the medical authorities were satisfied that I was no longer infectious and could be discharged. I returned to my billet to tell my roommates that I would soon be rejoining them, but not until after my seven days sick leave. "You lucky devil!" was the mildest comment that greeted this news. My fellow Armourers pointed out in very strong language that they had had extra duties, because of my absence due to some "kid's ailment". And they would expect some recompense in the form of a few beers on my return.

Thinking it unwise to prolong the conversation, I hurriedly packed and dashed off to the station to catch the evening train to Regina. The next day I went on to Saskatoon, where I was able to visit the friends I had spent time with a few weeks before. Again I stayed in a hotel, but saw the family most days, and as before they made me very welcome. My leave ended all too soon, and it was time to return to camp and resume my duties after an absence of more than a month.

Almost immediately on my return, and by now it was early March, there was a severe blizzard that lasted four days. Conditions were so bad the camp was cut off from the town for a couple of days, so we had no milk . . . Fortunately the cookhouse had enough food to last out. The snow was knee deep and drifts of twelve feet were reported.

Then suddenly on the fifth day it stopped, and immediately there were blue skies and brilliant sunshine. Snow ploughs worked continuously to clear the runways. It took several days and just as this job was nearly completed there was a sudden thaw. In a very short time there was floodwater and mud everywhere.

On the third day of the thaw an attempt was made to resume flying, but after a couple of aircraft turned over on the runways, fortunately without injuring the aircrew, it was abandoned. It was a full fortnight from the start of the blizzard before flying was resumed and during this time there was very little for the Armourers to do. We spent the time playing cards, darts or reading.

Once flying resumed the instructors were anxious to make up for lost time and we worked from seven in the morning until late at night.

During this busy period we lost the services of an Armourer who had a fight with a Service Policeman, and as a result was quickly whisked away to serve fourteen days detention. When I rather unwisely grumbled about the resultant extra work my fellow Armourers quickly reminded me of my long stay in hospital, with an "infantile disease that a child normally recovered from in a week", and then having the nerve to go on sick leave. I seriously regretted telling them how comfortable I had been in hospital, and what a great time I had on sick leave.

Eventually the busy period ended as one Training Course ended and a new intake of Trainees was awaited.

Going Home

At the beginning of April, I saw in Station Orders that I was to be included in the draft to return to the UK soon. I was due for a forty-eight hour pass and decided to go to Regina with a fellow Armourer to do some shopping and celebrate the news of our imminent return to England. We did the shopping, but our celebration was hampered by the complete absence of alcoholic drinks anywhere. We did not discover the reason. It was probably due to a strike.

On our way back to Weyburn our train hit a man on the line, we never found out if it was an accident or suicide. The train stopped and the body was brought into our carriage: a horrific and grisly ending to a disappointing stay in Regina.

★ ★ ★

On 22nd April 1943 I left Weyburn as a member of a draft of twenty Airmen to travel to RAF Moncton in New Brunswick, about 2,000 miles to the east. Moncton was an assembly point for drafts arriving and leaving Canada and was about a hundred miles from Halifax in Nova Scotia, the principal port on the east coast. Our first stop was at Regina where we had to catch a train going east. We had plenty of time to get a meal in a hotel; beer was still unobtainable so we had to make do with soft drinks, before boarding a late evening train to Winnipeg, where we arrived in the middle of the following day.

We had all recently been paid, so some of us decided to say farewell to the Prairie Provinces by having lunch at one of the principal hotels in the city — The Fort Garry.

Afterwards, we had time for a walk round the city and some sight seeing before boarding our train in the evening. That night and all the next day we travelled through the province of Ontario, seeing mainly forests and stopping at no town of any size. We had another night on the train before arriving at Montreal in the province of Quebec.

It was Easter Sunday and we could hear the bells of the Cathedral Of Notre Dame. We had a couple of hours before resuming our journey; some of us walked up the hill to look at the cathedral. A service had just started, but we were able to stand quietly at the back and enjoy the grandeur of this magnificent building and listen to the organ and the choir. Afterwards we had time for a quick look round the city before joining our train at mid-day.

We noticed that all the signs and advertisements were in French, the preferred language of the shopkeepers. Once more we set off in our train and travelled the rest of the day and through the night before eventually reaching our destination. We had been travelling for five days and four nights.

RAF Moncton was an enormous camp capable, we were told, of housing 10,000 service people. Apart from relatively few permanent staff all were transient personnel, either waiting to be put on a troopship to return to the UK or new arrivals waiting to be sent to various RAF stations in Canada. The accommodation was pretty basic, but we knew we wouldn't be there long; in fact it was three weeks.

The following day to my great delight, a draft of about 200 men arrived from North Battleford, and amongst them were a number of my friends. We had a reunion party in the canteen that night and drank a good deal of beer. This was the only place where alcohol could be bought as New Brunswick was a "dry" province; alcohol could not be bought anywhere outside the camp boundaries.

The days passed slowly. There was little to do apart from a few fatigues. We used to walk into the town quite often and have supper in one of the many restaurants. And sometimes we went to the cinema.

The countryside around the camp was green and pleasant and a complete contrast to the drabness of the prairies where we had been for the last two years. There were thousands of Airmen at the camp. Quite by chance I met up with a Frome lad who had just arrived from England. He was waiting for a posting to an Aircrew Training Course. After that one meeting I didn't see him again until many years later in Frome.

At last we got the news we were waiting for, and on the morning of May 16th we boarded a train to Halifax, which we reached that afternoon. All my friends from North Battleford were on the same draft.

We embarked on the 26,000-ton liner "Empress of Scotland"; it was formerly the "Empress of Japan". Its name was hurriedly changed after Pearl Harbour. It was more than twice the size of the ship that brought us to Canada two years previously.

We were told that we would travel unescorted, because our ship could travel at 22 knots and would be much faster than any U-boat we might encounter. We just hoped they were right and that the Germans had not designed any super fast versions recently.

Like most troop ships it was packed to capacity, and we were told that there were 4,000 Airmen on board. Conditions were better than on the troopship that brought us to Canada, but it still left a lot to be desired. We still slept in hammocks packed close together and the washing and toilet facilities were pretty basic. However, the knowledge that we were going home made us feel better about the conditions.

Our ship set off early the next morning, the sea was very calm and initially we glided along with hardly any motion, watching the Canadian coastline recede. On the second day there was a slight swell on the sea and many people became seasick including myself. Most of us had recovered by the next day, helped by the fact that the sea remained fairly calm.

We continued on our way in perfect weather, cloudless skies and warm sunshine and we were able to spend time sunbathing on deck. We were told that we were travelling well south, away from the normal shipping lanes, which was why we were enjoying such good weather. It seemed that we had the sea to ourselves; not another craft had been seen for two or three days.

On the fifth day an alert was sounded when an unidentified aircraft was sighted and there was some fear that it might be a Focke Wulf, the German long-range aircraft. Fortunately, it was an American Liberator that had been sent out to escort us.

The following day an RAF Sunderland aircraft escorted us. On the seventh day we saw the coast of Ireland and were greeted by a couple of Spitfire aircraft that flew overhead.

Next morning we docked at Liverpool and after passing through Customs, with only the most perfunctory of checks, we were taken to RAF West Kirby from whence we had departed some two years previously. Our sea crossing on our return had taken only seven days as opposed to eleven days in the S.S. Ruanhine on our outward journey.

CHAPTER
ELEVEN

Return to England

We only stayed at West Kirby for a couple of days, just long enough to be kitted out to what was called Home Scale, which meant being issued with items that we had not needed in Canada, such as respirators and steel helmets, and handing in our khaki drill. It was good to be back in England, even though we missed the bright lights of Canada and realized we would have to get accustomed once again to the dreary blackout. Our first few meals in the cookhouse reminded us that we would also miss the lavish catering we had enjoyed. On the other hand, it was nice to see the lush green countryside of England in May after the drabness of the prairie.

We were paid and issued with travel warrants, and then taken to Liverpool, where we could catch trains to our various destinations for our fourteen days leave. I had sent a telegram to say I was back in England and when I was likely to be returning home. I caught a train from Liverpool to Bristol and then a local train to Frome.

To my surprise another Airman who got into my carriage at Bristol was a former pupil at my old school. He was also on his way home on leave. We were able to reminisce on our journey. On arrival we went our different ways and I never saw him again. In the two years I had been away I had met no fewer than six Airmen from Frome that I had known previously. This seemed remarkable; Frome is quite a small town and the likelihood of meeting anyone I knew in the journey to and fro and in the vastness of Canada would seem fairly remote.

I arrived at Frome station at 11p.m. Eileen and my brother and brother-in-law met me. I was loaded down with kit bags and backpacks and was very grateful to be met, and that my brother had brought his van. I had two weeks very enjoyable leave, the big event being that Eileen and I became engaged on 29th May. We had exchanged letters on a weekly, and sometimes twice weekly basis and now wished to put our relationship on a permanent basis. We realized it was likely to be a long engagement, as we didn't intend to get married until I was demobbed and we could find a home of our own. It was to be almost four years before we married; I was not demobbed until the summer of 1946. And it was several more months before I was settled in a job and we were able to find a place to live.

We went to the local jeweller to buy an engagement ring. Due to wartime restrictions there were only two to choose from; fortunately there was one we liked. During my leave we had several parties to celebrate our engagement and my return. My cousins from Chippenham came for a weekend to join in the celebrations, which went on and on.

One day Eileen and I cycled to Horningsham to see my old boss and he persuaded us to stay for a dance in the village hall. This went on until nearly midnight. We left our bicycles and he drove us home, though more than slightly inebriated: no breath tests in those days. The bicycles were delivered the next day by one of the estate lorries, quite contrary to the petrol regulations at that time.

Eileen and I also had a day in Bristol. My mother accompanied us so she could visit relatives, but instead we went to Bristol Hippodrome where Henry Hall and his band were appearing. This was a very well known band both before and after the war and could be heard regularly on the radio. We were quite thrilled to see such well-known performers, but were appalled to see the amount of bomb damage in Bristol.

My fourteen days' leave came to an end and I had still not received notification of where I should report. This pleased me greatly and I enjoyed the extra days' leave. Eventually my posting notice arrived on the morning of Whit Monday telling me to report immediately to RAF Lindholme near Doncaster. As it was a bank holiday I thought the next day would do, and enjoyed that final day with Eileen. I caught the first train to London, changed for Doncaster and on arriving found there was transport to Lindholme, about eight miles away. I reported in at about seven o'clock that evening, a day late; nobody seemed to mind.

RAF Lindholme

The next morning after breakfast I reported to the Armoury and learned that we were part of a new unit forming up, and would soon be leaving Lindholme for an undisclosed destination. As there did not seem to be much to do I walked round the hangars and looked at several large four-engine aircraft parked there. I had learned that they were Lancaster and Halifax bombers, which had been introduced into service since I left England two years ago. They were indeed huge compared with the Ansons and Harvards I had worked on in Canada.

I could see there were two types of aircraft, but didn't know which was a Lancaster and which a Halifax. Unwilling to confess to such ignorance I climbed into an aircraft, looked at its documentation and learned it was a Halifax. I then knew that the others were Lancasters. Feeling a little more knowledge-able I returned to the Armoury wondering how I could learn about gun turrets etc. that had not been included in my Bomb Armourers course.

The next day I met up with Jack and Peter who had not only been fellow Armourers at North Battleford, but also good friends. To celebrate our reunion we walked to the village of Hatfield, a mile or so away, and had a few drinks in the village pub.

There was very little work for us to do while the unit was forming up so we were told to attend a week's Defence Course to be held in the camp; one way, I suppose, of keeping us occupied. We duly reported and found an alarmingly enthusiastic Sergeant running it, from the RAF regiment. We feared that there might be an assault course that would demonstrate our unfitness. We needn't have worried, it was mostly to do with firing various weapons and as Armourers we had more experience than the other course members, and were able to show off a little and did.

The course included grenade throwing that was new to us. We did this with great circumspection, keeping a wary eye on our companions in case they dropped one and we needed to make a speedy exit. We also had to go through the gas chamber without respirators to experience a certain type of gas. Needless to say we did this at top speed; even so we emerged coughing and spluttering. This seemed a lunatic exercise akin to hitting your head against a wall to experience how nice it is when you stop.

One night after the course, I was detailed for guard duty on the airfield. Two of us patrolled armed with Sten guns looking out for intruders, fortunately we didn't see any. The guard was organised on a two hours on four hours off basis: two hours patrolling followed by four hours resting in the guard hut — a Nissan Hut on the edge of the airfield furnished with a few beds, no blankets as we would be resting fully clothed. For refreshments we were provided with a bucket of cocoa from the cookhouse and a few sandwiches.

When we returned to the hut for our four hours' rest, we noticed as we drank the tepid cocoa and chewed on the dry sandwiches that the hut was infested with field mice. There were plenty of crumbs on the floor and the local mouse population obviously regarded this hut as a very desirable fast food establishment. When we saw some scurrying across the beds we decided it would be prudent to tuck our trouser legs into our socks before lying down in case an adventurous mouse decided to explore our legs.

We managed to get a couple of hours' sleep before it was time to go on guard again, and were not molested by the mice.

RAF Faldingworth

After a couple of weeks at Lindholme we were told that we were to go to a new RAF station at Faldingworth in Lincolnshire. Jack and I were in the Advance Party, and early in July we set off in a small convoy of lorries to make the two-hour journey to our new camp. When we arrived we were far from impressed. The camp was obviously not finished and workmen were still busy on it. Furthermore, it seemed miles from anywhere; for the last few miles we had travelled on minor roads with few signs of habitation.

The camp had engulfed a farm, situated right in the middle of it, with the airfield and hangars one side, and living quarters — Nissan Huts — the other. The farm was still occupied and the family still farming the fields not taken over by the RAF. Ironically the son of the farmer was in the RAF and came home on leave to an active RAF airfield.

Our Advance Party consisted of about fifty or sixty Airmen, with a couple of Sergeants and a Warrant Officer in charge. We assembled to receive instructions and were further depressed when the Warrant Officer said that for the time being we had no cook, and asked for volunteers to man the Cookhouse. Three rather scruffy Airmen quickly volunteered. When we saw who they were we suspected the reason they had volunteered was not a wish to demonstrate their culinary skills, but rather an opportunity to make off with rationed items such as tea and butter, and sell them in the local pub. One of them claimed to have been a cook on a trawler. We hoped at least he might be good at cooking fish. We had been given packed meals for the day so we wouldn't find out how well they cooked until the next day.

The next news that lowered our spirits further was that the toilets were not finished and our first job was to construct temporary ones. This did not take long. A level piece of ground was chosen fairly close to the Nissan Huts, and some latrine buckets off-loaded from a lorry and arranged in a circle. Lavatory seats were balanced uncertainly on the buckets and a canvas screen, at about shoulder height, constructed round them. An Airman who asked what would happen when it rained got the terse reply, "We get wet."

Then to the Nissan Huts to make our beds, this meant collecting bedsteads, mattresses, blankets — no sheets, of course — and putting them together. This was to be my first experience of living in Nissan Huts; I would continue to do so for most of the rest of the war. The huts accommodated about a dozen beds down each side, over which there was an overhead shelf for some of our possessions, though most had to be kept in our kitbags. A stove in the centre of the hut was the only source of heat, its effectiveness depended on the amount of fuel we could obtain. We got used to living in these dormitories and the complete lack of privacy, and regarded them as reasonably comfortable for wartime living.

On our first evening, Jack and I decided to seek out the nearest pub, which turned out to be at Faldingworth village some two miles away. We enjoyed our drink, but it was a long way and we were footsore when we returned to camp.

We had two or three weeks at Faldingworth, waiting for the rest of the Unit to arrive and it was a mixture of frenzied activity — unloading lorries etc. — or sheer boredom with nothing to do. Our volunteer cooks fed us in a rough and ready, and rather unhygienic, way. They smoked most of the time while preparing meals, adding tobacco ash to most ingredients.

Breakfast was always lumpy porridge and perhaps overcooked sausages. Lunch was often some kind of stew. We thought it best not to ask what went into it, particularly when someone said he hadn't seen the farm cat lately that used to hang around the cookhouse looking for scraps. A pessimist thought the scraps might have poisoned it. The evening meal could be baked beans and the sweet a slab of cake, known as yellow peril, soaked in watery custard.

There was a complete transformation when a Sergeant Cook and some trained cooks were posted in. It turned out that the Sergeant had been a chef at a hotel in civilian life. We were soon enjoying really first-class meals. At about the same time, the proper toilets were finished and we were grateful that we no longer had to use the open-air facilities with their wobbly seats.

On one never to be forgotten occasion, we walked the two miles to the pub in Faldingworth only to find it was closed with a "Sold Out" notice displayed. Occasionally we went to Lincoln, but it always seemed to be packed with troops, RAF and Army, and it was difficult to get into cinemas or pubs.

One weekend Jack and I had a leave pass so we went to Nottingham and stayed overnight in a very run-down YMCA Hostel. We were advised to put any valuables under our pillows while we slept, and even to stand the feet of the beds in our boots to ensure they weren't stolen. We didn't make that journey again.

When the rest of the Unit arrived and our Lancaster bombers flew in we were able to function as 1667 Heavy Conversion Unit (HCU). Our purpose was to train Aircrew that had been using twin engined aircraft, like Wellingtons, to fly the four-engined Lancasters, which could be used on operations if needed.

We soon got into the routine of an Armament Section in a busy Unit; cleaning and fitting the Browning machine guns, checking the gun turrets, loading up practice bombs, flares, ammunition . . . There was night flying, when we loaded up and checked the aircraft, and then waited in a flight hut on the edge of the airfield with other ground crew for the aircraft to return. It was a very dispersed site; the aircraft could be parked a couple of miles away from our living quarters. We used bikes or got lifts in a station lorry. This was the time of the great RAF bomber offensive and nearly every night the sky would be full of Lancaster and Halifax Bombers from the many RAF stations in Lincolnshire.

There were one or two mishaps. Once a practice smoke bomb fell off into the bomb bay of an aircraft as it was taking off and filled the aircraft with smoke. Fortunately it was able to make an emergency landing without damage or casualties.

On another occasion an Armourer working on a machine gun in the front turret of a Lancaster inadvertently fired off a burst of rounds that went uncomfortably near the car of the commanding officer making a tour of the airfield. The car screeched to a halt and the CO came rocketing out to seek the culprit. The Armourer's explanation that he had forgotten to put the guns on safe before pressing the trigger did little to mollify him.

Later on the Armourer told us that he was on a promotion board at the end of the week. "I bet I don't get it now," he said.

He didn't.

There were not many places to go on our day off. Once a couple of Armourers decided to make the trip to Grimsby. There was an infrequent bus service from the village, but they managed to get there all right. They did some shopping and then had a leisurely if rather liquid lunch before getting an afternoon bus back, because they were on duty that night. The bus was full of ladies who had been shopping and also a female driver. As the vehicle made its slow progress along the country roads the Airmen began to regret their third and fourth pints. They desperately needed a toilet.

Eventually they plucked up courage to ask the driver if she would stop and let them get out and wait for them, as there was not another bus for five hours. Rather grudgingly she did and the, by then, really desperate Airmen dashed out, scrambled over the gate and sought refuge behind the hedge, well aware of the disapproving stares of the other occupants of the bus. In their haste they stepped into a couple of large cowpats, and on their return they brought with them the unwelcome smell of cow manure. For the rest of the journey they huddled down in their seats and at Faldingworth they gratefully left the bus, trying to avoid the gaze of the other passengers. When we heard their story we decided that a trip to Grimsby was for teetotallers only.

For the remaining months of the year it was routine work in this rather bleak Lincolnshire airfield where it always seemed to be both cold and wet. Leave was very much looked forward to, and I had a week in October, which I much enjoyed.

Soon we were into Christmas and the traditional RAF Christmas Dinner. This was my third and I wondered how many more there would be; there seemed no prospect of an early end to the war.

CHAPTER
TWELVE

1944

The first few months passed uneventfully with us being fully employed on routine work on the Lancasters. Occasionally we had to do some testing in the air, which just meant a quick flight round the airfield. From time to time we took turns at airfield guard duty; two of us patrolling the airfield at night, armed with Sten guns, looking out for intruders. We never saw any.

One diversion was provided at an encampment of wooden huts on the edge of the airfield; it housed Irish labourers who were working on one of the runways. They had a canteen where, given we did not call too late, we could buy a mug of tea and delicious ham sandwiches made with fresh bread and plenty of ham. This was much better than the miserly fare produced for the guard by the Cookhouse, which generally consisted of some rather dry spam sandwiches and a bucket of cocoa. The latter stood on the stove in the hut to keep warm and gradually thickened as the night wore on.

Reinforced by the refreshments obtained from our Irish friends we resumed the patrol, keeping an eye out for the Orderly Officer who sometimes turned out to check the guard. When it was dark, he generally did this with some circumspection; he knew the patrol had live ammunition and might have little experience with the notoriously unpredictable Sten guns.

The weather seemed to be continually cold and damp, and sometimes foggy, grounding the aircraft. It was always a struggle to keep our Nissan Hut warm. At night illegal raids would be made on the fuel dumps and a few buckets of coke carried off to replenish the supplies in our hut.

One day in March, I was told I was to go on an Armourers Conversion Course, at the end of which I would no longer be just a Bomb Armourer, but a fully trained General Armourer. As I had been working on guns for nearly two years I would be going over old ground. I had to obey orders, so I packed my kit, said goodbye to my friends, and made my way to RAF Kirkham in Lancaster.

RAF Kirkham

RAF Kirkham was situated close to the main road from Preston to Blackpool, about mid way between the two. It was a typical training camp not unlike RAF Melksham where I did my initial stint, and we were quite comfortably housed in wooden huts. Several of us arrived at the same time. Our course did not start for a few days; we were informed that in the meantime we would be employed on fatigues. The relish with which the Flight Sergeant delivered this information made us a bit apprehensive about the immediate future.

The very next day we were sent to Preston Barracks to collect rations for our cookhouse. We were quite curious to see what our food looked like before the RAF cooks got their hands on it; we boarded a lorry and set off. On arrival we drew up alongside a large building and went in. It was a cold store for meat and other items. A short, heavily built store-man unhooked a side of beef from a rack and, to my horror, put it on my shoulder and told me to load it onto the lorry.

It was so heavy I could feel my knees buckling under the weight. I made a few staggering steps towards the door bent double and with my legs trembling. Just as I was about to collapse under this great load a fellow Airman came to my assistance and together we managed to put it on the lorry. The store man looked on disparagingly, and said it shouldn't take two men to do one man's work. When we looked at the weight ticket, 100 lbs, we didn't feel too bad about it.

We loaded up the rest of the meat, unashamedly working in pairs. The Airman who came to my rescue said when the meat was put on my shoulder my eyes nearly popped out, and I staggered around bent double making funny little mooing noises. He was afraid I might be injured and they would be one man short, which is why he was so quick to assist.

The rest of the week passed without incident and the fatigues, though boring, were not too demanding, and soon we assembled in the classroom to start our course. Some of the other members, like myself, had plenty of practical experience working on guns, so it was generally only the theory we needed to absorb.

We were allowed out of camp in the evenings, and also Saturday and Sunday afternoons, providing we had not been detailed for Guard Duty or Fire Patrol.

There was a bus stop right outside the camp gate for frequent buses to Preston and Blackpool, our preferred choice as during this period Blackpool had a very fine football team: they were able to draw on former professional footballers serving in the Army and RAF stationed in the many camps in the area. I watched them several times and almost all the Blackpool players were internationals, including the legendary Stanley Matthews. This was a class of football completely new to me; I had previously only watched locals at Frome, and very occasionally the Bristol team.

After the match we could walk along the promenade and visit the Blackpool Tower, and perhaps listen to the organ played by Sandy MacPherson, who we knew from his regular programmes on the radio. Occasionally, on a fine Sunday afternoon we would visit nearby Lytham St. Annes and listen to the band playing in the park, and afterwards have tea and cakes at a Salvation Army Canteen.

Eileen had given me the address of her great aunt who lived close by; I would also visit her on some Sunday afternoons. I was very kindly received and given tea and cakes. All in all my life at Kirkham was quite pleasant. I just wondered where I would be sent when the course finished.

One event disturbed my routine. We were told that all course students would take part in a parade through Preston the following Saturday. This was to support a fund raising event in aid of the war effort called "Wings for Victory". The authorities rather optimistically thought that the citizens of Preston would be so impressed by the sight of a large contingent of Airmen marching through their streets they would give generously to the fund and fill the many collecting boxes.

A few days before the event we assembled on the Parade Ground and were addressed by the Station Warrant Officer. In an attempt to prevent us from disgracing the RAF too much when we appeared in public, he had kindly arranged for us to practice marching each evening until Saturday, and under his personal supervision. Each evening we marched around the Parade Ground whilst being shouted at and generally insulted by several Sergeants and the Station Warrant Officer. On the last evening we were finally dismissed with the unflattering comment, "Thank God we've got an army."

The next day we were conveyed to Preston in lorries, with our buttons brightly polished and boots shiny. There we formed up in columns of three, ready to march off, with a band and one or two officers in front and NCOs in the rear. The band struck up and off we went, concentrating on keeping in step. During this march I witnessed an example of sheer effrontery and opportunism that I have always remembered.

We had been marching a little while, watched by a scattering of civilians, and were just rounding a corner when a double-decker bus slowly passed us. To my utter astonishment the Airman in front of me quickly stepped on the bus, went upstairs and disappeared from view. I waited to hear shouts of rage from the NCOs, but nothing happened. No one in authority had noticed. The Airman in the middle rank stepped to one side to fill the gap and we continued like this until the end of the march. I never discovered whether he rejoined us while we waited for our transport at the end of the march or made his own way back to camp. I marvelled at the sheer nerve of the man and have often wondered what a quick thinking and supreme opportunist like that became when he returned to civilian life.

As we were coming to the end of our course we received news of the D-Day landings in France. This was encouraging: it gave us hope that the end of the war in Europe might not be too far off. A few days later we got less welcome news that no leave would be granted at the end of the course, and we would return straight away to our previous units. I had mixed feelings about returning to Faldingworth; I had hoped I might be posted to an RAF station nearer home. On the other hand, I realised I could be sent much further away. On balance there was much to be said for returning to a unit I knew and where I had long-standing friends, some from my North Battleford days.

One of our course members was delighted to be returning to his previous unit. After his initial training, about three years previously, he had been posted to an RAF station only two miles from his home. He had established quite a cosy routine of cycling home after he had finished work and staying overnight when he wasn't on duty. He had been quite certain that at the end of this course he would have been posted elsewhere, perhaps even overseas, and to his delight he could now look forward to resuming his previous arrangements. He may well have continued until the end of the war.

When the course results were announced I was pleased to hear that I had marks of well over 80%. If it had not been the requirement to return all personnel to their units I might have been invited to stay at Kirkham as an instructor. I packed my kit and returned to Faldingworth, only to be told on my arrival that soon we were to move again to a new camp at Sandtoft some thirty miles away.

RAF Sandtoft

Sandtoft was a hamlet consisting of a few houses and a public house situated on a crossroads: only just in Yorkshire, the county boundary was close by, equidistant from Doncaster, Yorkshire, and Scunthorpe, Lincolnshire, each roughly twelve miles away.

The newly built RAF Station engulfed this tiny place. On one side were the living quarters, Nissan

Huts, the Cookhouse, NAAF . . . and on the other the airfield, hangars, workshops . . . Several hundred Airmen arrived and took up residence in the huts. Lorries and other vehicles came in and Lancaster and Halifax Bombers landed on the airfield. The change to their formerly quiet little backwater must have been traumatic.

The local pub probably sold more beer in a night than they had previously done in a month, and it says much for the supplier that they managed to cope with the increased demand. The hangars and workshops were more than a mile from the living quarters, and the aircraft dispersed around the airfield a further mile or so away. Because of these distances we were all issued with bicycles, sturdy upright machines painted khaki to show they were Government Property. We found them useful, not only for getting to work, but also for visiting pubs in outlying villages in the evenings. The land was very flat, ideal for cycling.

We were used to Nissan Hut accommodation and made the best of it. The ablutions for washing were not good. They were more than a hundred yards away, which was a nuisance when it was wet. And the supply of hot water was spasmodic. The adjoining showers were dismal, cold and uninviting. The toilets were quite near our hut, but there was no main drainage. Once again we had latrine buckets with wooden seats, but at least there was a roof, which was better than Faldingworth.

Every day an elderly man driving a horse and cart came round and emptied the buckets tipping them into large containers in the cart. He seemed undeterred by the awful smells and the slops that went on his clothes. And we often saw him sitting on his cart having his morning snack.

The latrine buckets tended to get rather full by the evening and I remember one occasion when some of our roommates came back from the pub having had too much to drink. One of them felt sick and dashed out to the toilet. He returned a little later and then suddenly clutched his mouth and said, "My teeth!" He returned to the toilet rolling his sleeve up well, but couldn't remember which bucket he had used. No one offered to help him and he was gone a long time. He eventually retrieved his dentures after exploring the noxious contents of several buckets, and discovered, too late, that he had forgotten to take his wristwatch off.

Then he went to the ablutions for a good wash — teeth, himself and wristwatch — in cold water, which was all that was available. He eventually returned to our hut a dishevelled and still slightly smelly person, until someone gave him a bottle of disinfectant to sprinkle on. That helped a bit.

We soon got into the routine of work at our new station. The airfield was so big that one dispersal site was quite close to the next village. During quiet periods it was tempting to take it in turns to pop into the pub for a quick drink. Because of the distance everyone cycled, at meal times there would be stacks of cycles outside the Cookhouse.

It was an open camp with no perimeter fence; the site was too large. Consequently, there was no check on the time Airmen came back to their billets at night or indeed if they returned at all. The essential requirement was to be at work at the correct time in the morning and be prompt in reporting for all other duties — such as night work as required, Airfield Guard . . .

No leave had been allowed immediately after the D-Day Landings. Later in the summer there was some relaxation and forty-eight hour passes were granted. They were normally from after duty on Friday until midnight Sunday, but they could be stretched a little from early afternoon on Friday until reporting for work at 8 a.m. on Monday.

Even so this was not really enough time to go to Frome. However, Eileen had relations in Walsall she could stay with and meeting her there would more than halve my travelling time. We arranged a mutually convenient weekend and I got a leave pass and set off for Walsall. I caught a train from Doncaster to Sheffield, changed there for Birmingham and took a local train to Walsall. This worked successfully and we had a good weekend together at Eileen's aunt and uncle's.

My return journey was not so successful. I reached Sheffield early in the evening to discover there were no more trains until the next morning. I thought quickly, and remembered there was a bus service to Doncaster from Rotherham; there were trams from Sheffield to Rotherham, which was only six miles away. Off I went to the tram stop and was soon bumping and lurching on an old tram past several steel works on my way to Rotherham. There I discovered that indeed there was a bus service to Doncaster, but the last bus had gone and there wouldn't be another one that night.

I was contemplating this bad news when I noticed a young WAAF girl also studying the timetable and looking rather disconsolate. We chatted; she was also stationed at Sandtoft and had the same problem as me. We decided that the best thing to do was to return to Sheffield, catch the early morning train and hope we could get a lift from Doncaster to Sandtoft. So back we went to Sheffield and spent a long night on an empty station platform. We talked a lot and dozed a little until, at long last, our early morning train arrived. This got us to Doncaster at about 6.30 a.m. The next problem was how to get to Sandtoft, as we knew there was no bus service.

Outside the station we saw a lorry laden with milk churns. We talked to the driver who said he would go within a couple of miles of the camp. He had to stop at one or two farms on the way, but we were welcome to go with him. There seemed no likelihood of a better offer so we climbed up into the lorry to find there was only one seat. The driver grinned and said, "I don't expect you mind sharing," so that's what we did. The girl sat on my lap as we travelled up and down farm lanes being barked at by farm dogs and to the accompaniment of the clanking of churns on the back of the lorry.

Eventually we were dropped off as promised. By this time it was 7.30 a.m. We started walking, knowing we couldn't reach camp by 8 a.m. We had only taken a few steps when a large army lorry drew up beside us. It was taking Italian prisoners of war to work at a farm and the driver said he could drop us off right outside our camp if we didn't mind getting in the back with the Ities. No one in the front of the lorry offered to give his place to my companion, so we had to clamber over the tailboard at the back. This was difficult for the WAAF as she was not very tall. She had to hitch up her skirt and while the Italians pulled from the top I pushed from the rear. During this operation I couldn't help noticing that her knickers didn't seem to be the official WAAF issue, which I thought was rather daring. It has to be said, when she set out on this journey she didn't know they would be seen by a previously unknown Airman and several Italians.

We were only in the lorry a few minutes, during which time there was much animated chatter among the Italians, none of which we could understand, and also plenty of flashing smiles. We were lowered from the lorry right outside the camp, and it was only a quarter to eight. With a hasty goodbye we scuttled off on our separate ways, and I don't remember ever seeing her again.

My friends Jack and Peter who had been with me in North Battleford were also at Sandtoft and as they were both Armourers I saw them quite frequently and we often went out together. Soon after arriving at Sandtoft we made another friend, Bill. He was in his early forties, quite a bit older than us, and had only recently joined up — probably in the oldest age group to be conscripted.

We met him while having a drink in the NAAFI, and he told us he wasn't very happy in his Nissan Hut, as some of the occupants were very rowdy. I knew there was a vacant place in a hut near us and he was able to occupy that to his complete satisfaction. We learned that he came from Glasgow, was married with three children and had a business in partnership with his brother. His job at Sandtoft was a Junior Clerk in the Orderly Room, but he was so efficient that he was soon pretty well running it. And the Officer In Charge, who was young enough to be Bill's son, and also from Glasgow, came to rely on him not only in his official capacity, but also for advice on other matters.

Much later in our acquaintance we came to realise that Bill was quite wealthy. He rented rooms in the village during the school holidays so his family could join him, and when he went home on leave he paid extra to travel First Class. He was never ostentatious, though once when we were with him in Doncaster he said he would treat us to tea. But instead of going to the YMCA he went into a big hotel, and with great aplomb ordered afternoon tea and was quite at ease, whereas we felt slightly out of place. He was a good companion and readily joined us in our trips to the village pub.

To digress a little, because of his age etc. he was demobbed before me. We always kept in touch by an exchange of Christmas cards and an accompanying note. Some twenty years after I was demobbed I had to go to Glasgow on business, so I got in touch with Bill and suggested we meet. I had an enthusiastic response and he arranged to pick me up from my hotel. This he did and took me to his home, which was a large house on the outskirts of Glasgow standing in its own grounds, and with an impressive in and out drive. I met his wife and we had drinks in a very elegant lounge before adjourning to the dining room where we had a nice meal, and a servant waited on us. It was a memorable evening and Bill was very enthusiastic when talking about our RAF days. I continued to keep in touch over the next years, but inevitably in view of the difference in our ages eventually I had a note saying that he had died.

As we had bicycles we could visit neighbouring villages on our off-duty evenings and sample the local beer. One of the Armourers was a pianist, and sometimes a little group of us went with him to a pub with a piano where we would have a singsong, and he would get free beer. He would play all the favourite wartime songs and there would be enthusiastic, if rather raucous, singing. His party piece was the Warsaw Concerto, which featured in a well-known film at the time entitled "Dangerous Moonlight". We listened in respectful silence as he demonstrated his skilful playing and applauded loudly at the end.

However, he soon reverted to popular songs and sometimes, as the evening wore on, to rather bawdy favourites such as "Quartermasters Stores" or "Roll Me Over". When the pub closed we cycled rather uncertainly back to camp singing on the way, alarming the cattle in adjoining fields. One hazard was a deep ditch alongside the road, into which occasionally a drunken Airman would disappear and have to be pulled out. If anyone got a puncture two Airmen would wobble along on one bike and another would try and manage his own bike, plus the unrideable one.

Someone discovered a farm where the farmer's wife would serve bacon and egg supper and home-made pudding, all of which were rationed items. This became a favourite venue when we were in funds.

We normally had one day off in ten, and two or three of us would often go to Doncaster. Our first stop would be at the municipal baths where for payment of about a shilling we could have the use of a private bathroom. The camp shower room was dreadful, with irregular supplies of hot water and the concrete floor often two or three inches deep in water due to blocked drains.

A bath with unlimited supplies of hot water was a luxury to be savoured leisurely, and we normally spent at least an hour in it. Weekday mornings were not a busy time in the baths, so we weren't pressed to leave. There was a blue mark round the bath to denote the five inches of water officially allowed, but we disregarded this assuming it only applied to civilians. After all we were British Servicemen and the newspapers told us we were engaged in a desperate battle against the foe.

Admittedly things weren't too desperate at Sandtoft, apart from the shower room, and the only foe we had seen so far were Italian prisoners of war working at a neighbouring farm.

As we soaked in our hot tubs with water nearly up to our chins we thought how good it was for our morale and believed that the Service Authorities would surely approve. Eventually emerging from our luxury baths we would go to lunch at a Salvation Army Canteen, spend the afternoon at a cinema and then have tea. We had time in the evening for a drink in one of the many pubs in Doncaster before catching a bus back to camp, and would consider we had had a good day out.

Our bicycles were a great boon both for work and leisure. They were sturdy, heavy machines and not much went wrong with them, apart from an occasional puncture, which we could mend in the armoury. As they could be "borrowed" without the owner's knowledge — generally by Aircrew who were not issued with bicycles, it was prudent to use a padlock if they had to be left anywhere.

One failing was that in very cold weather the gears would freeze and the chain would turn without engaging, but this could easily be remedied by pouring on a little warm water. This we didn't have. Fortunately nature provided an alternative ... This worked perfectly and we could cycle off to breakfast.

There was very little "in camp" entertainment. We had no Station Concert Party and an ENSA Concert Party never visited us. Occasionally there was a film show in the NAAFI, where again we sat on our pillows; there was a row of chairs for officers and senior NCOs. On one occasion we had a film starring Betty Grable who was a favourite "pin-up" of the time, and, in Service Camps all over the world, there were many pictures of her wearing a swimsuit. Not a bikini as they had not yet been invented.

The climax of this particular film was Betty wearing a very revealing dress and crooning a somewhat provocative song entitled "Cuddle Up a Little Closer". As she advanced nearer and nearer to the camera she almost filled the screen and a howl of delight, or perhaps desire, went up from the hundred or so Airmen in the audience. The few WAAF who were there looked a little nervous and the officers seated in the front row turned round disapprovingly. This was the high point of the show from the Airmen's point of view and the remainder was an anti-climax. At the end of the film the WAAF grouped together and rapidly scuttled off to their billets.

Isolated as we were in a remote part of Yorkshire we saw nothing of the bombing of British cities by the Germans, and knew only what fellow Airmen from those parts told us when they returned from leave. One night we did get a glimpse of a German "terror weapon". On this particular evening we were in our Nissan Hut when we heard a noise that seemed very different from normal aircraft flying overhead.

We went outside. In the sky we saw what seemed to be several small aircraft, each with a flickering flame coming from its exhaust. A Londoner with us immediately said, "They are Doodle Bombs." This was the common name for the V1 Flying Bombs first launched against London in June. Up to now they had only been used against London and the Southern

Counties, as that had been the limit of their range. We watched until they disappeared from view and wondered whether the Germans had now managed to increase the range and we would be seeing more of them.

Because of censorship nothing was reported in the newspapers or radio, and it was only long afterwards that we learned that these flying bombs had been launched from aircraft flying over the North Sea; the aim had been to hit Liverpool or Manchester.

Much later still we were told that most of them fell in open country and did little damage, but tragically one dropped on a house in which a party was being held and everyone was killed. The V1s were never used in this way again, but continued to be used against London and the Southern Counties until the British Army captured the launching sites.

I had a week's leave in October, which enabled me to go to Frome and spend time with Eileen and my family. I enjoyed the visit, but realised I would not be going home again for another four or five months.

Early in December both Jack and I had a forty-eight hour pass. Not enough for either of us to get home, but we wanted to do something other than stay in camp. We thought it would be nice to stay in a hotel for a couple of nights, and as Scunthorpe was the nearest town we decided to go there. It was not difficult to book a room.

Known principally for its iron and steel industries, the town was far from being a holiday destination.

We caught a bus to Scunthorpe on Friday afternoon and arrived at our hotel in time for an evening meal. We shared a room to cut down on cost and were well pleased with our accommodation: a good-sized room with two comfortable single beds. After our meal we went to a cinema and on our return had a drink in the hotel lounge, enjoying the luxury of comfortable armchairs. At about 11p.m. when we were thinking of going to bed a group of men came in chattering and laughing among themselves quite loudly, and generally behaving in a rather extrovert way. Nowadays they would have been described as "camp", but then the word only meant a collection of huts or tents.

I was very interested; I had never seen the like in Frome. Jack, who was much more worldly wise than I, leaned over and whispered. I was quite surprised and asked, "Do you really think so?"

Jack impatiently replied, "Of course I think so, it's b—— obvious!" He then added somewhat rudely, I thought, "At least it's obvious to anyone who hasn't spent most of his life on a farm in Somerset."

I watched the little group with renewed interest and presently two of them came over and sat near us. They were quite friendly and we were soon in conversation. They were in a Touring Concert Party called "We Were In The Forces", and were appearing in the Scunthorpe Theatre. I saw Jack had difficulty in keeping a straight face when he heard the title of the show, and told me afterwards that he had a pretty good idea why they were no longer in the Forces.

A little while later we excused ourselves and went to bed, and when we were in our room Jack said we should lock our door. But there was no key, nor was there a bolt; we decided to put a chair behind the door. We got off to sleep all right, but in the night I woke up and needed to go to the toilet. It was very dark and I immediately fell over the chair we had put by the door, and staggering back I bumped into Jack's bed and woke him. He shouted out; he thought there was an intruder in our room.

I managed to find the light switch and we sorted ourselves out, though Jack was not best pleased at being woken up and called me a clumsy clot.

The next day we explored Scunthorpe; we didn't find it very exciting. We saw the theatre where our fellow hotel guests were performing. We decided we had time to see their show and booked seats for that evening, not too near the front in case they recognised us. We did enjoy it and it was funny. Many of the jokes were very rude, though that seemed to go down well with the audience.

Most of the all-male cast dressed as women and very realistic they were, too. When we returned to our hotel there was no sign of the theatricals nor did we see them at breakfast so perhaps they were already on their way to the next venue. Later that day we returned to Sandtoft having enjoyed our weekend in the hotel. Not that we could say that Scunthorpe in December was very exciting.

We remembered the concert party and wondered if any of them did well in show business.

★   ★   ★

Generally, the remaining weeks of 1944 passed uneventfully. There was some excitement when late one afternoon a number of American Flying Fortress Bombers, returning from a daylight raid, landed on our airfield. Due to fog at their own base they had been diverted. With great interest we watched these unfamiliar aircraft land one after the other, and taxi to one of the Dispersal Flights.

Transport was sent to bring the Aircrew to our Domestic Site. Special arrangements had to be made to feed them and provide overnight accommodation.

That evening most of them found their way to our village pub, which was packed, and our American guests provided quite a lively evening. Next morning they were able to return to their own airfields and we watched them as they flew away.

Then it was Christmas again and time for an RAF Christmas dinner with officers and NCOs waiting on the Airmen. This was my fourth. As always on these occasions we speculated on how many more we would have. The war in Europe seemed to be reaching its final stages, with the Allied forces advancing in the west and the Russians in the east. However, the war against Japan seemed as if it would go on for a long time. We knew nothing about the atom bomb.

CHAPTER
THIRTEEN

1945

The first non-routine event of the year for me happened one February afternoon when, with another Armourer I was told to report to the Armament Officer. One of our Lancaster aircraft had crashed some twenty or thirty miles away. An ambulance had been sent, but he understood there were no survivors. No bombs were being carried as it was just a training flight, but there were guns and ammunition that needed to be removed if possible. This was to be our job. He also thought we should stay overnight to "keep an eye on things", and to ensure the wreckage was not tampered with by "unauthorised personnel".

Rather disconsolately we returned to our huts and put on our warmest clothing; fortunately we were enjoying a spell of fairly mild weather.

When we returned to the Armoury to collect Sten guns — we were meant to be guards — we had to put up with some unsympathetic banter from our fellow Armourers: "Watch out for ghosts!" "Try not to shoot yourselves!" and everyone was certain that there would soon be snow.

The aircraft had crashed into rising ground in a wood, it was some way off the road and we had to get there by lorry up a rough track. Remains were scattered over a large area, and trees and branches had been broken in its descent. There had been a fire, now extinguished, and the sickly smell of burning persisted. A small working party under the supervision of a Sergeant was doing some preliminary clearing up, and they were surprised to see us.

There had only been three crewmembers and an ambulance had taken away their remains that morning. The working party had been scouring the area, picking up small pieces of wreckage they could take back in the lorry. The Sergeant laughed when I mentioned the guns; they were twisted almost beyond recognition and would have to be cut away from the wreckage, which we were clearly unable to do. We joined the working party and picked up some rounds of ammunition, and a signal pistol that was still intact. I also found a collar and a boot, and hesitated to pick it up in case there was a foot in it; fortunately there was not.

When it started to get dark the Sergeant said he would be taking his men back to camp. In the morning, he would return to meet a working party from a Maintenance Unit. They would be bringing low-loader lorries and lifting equipment to clear the site completely. A tent had been rigged up for temporary shelter, and he would leave that for us.

I looked round at the scattered bits of wreckage and asked if that was all there was to guard. He shrugged, "Well, if your Officer told you to stay all night you will just have to stay." However, he helpfully told us there was a farm cottage a few hundred yards away, and the lady had been very friendly and brought them a drink. After suggesting we call on them he said, "Cheerio, see you in the morning," and departed with his Working Party leaving us alone in the fading light, looking at the scattered remains of the Lancaster aircraft.

We set off down the path to find the fore-mentioned cottage. After walking for a while we reached it and knocked on the door. A middle-aged lady answered; after introductions she invited us in and we met her husband. They couldn't wait to tell us about the crash landing within half a mile of their cottage. Interrupting the flow of conversation, she offered to make us a drink and get something for us to eat. We had food, but were glad of hot drinks. Soon we were cosily sitting round the fire munching our sandwiches and drinking tea, and listening to further episodes from the drama of the previous night.

Eventually, we explained what our duties were, and the lady was very concerned. "Oh, you poor boys, fancy having to be on duty until tomorrow morning." We welcomed this expression of sympathy, which had been completely lacking from our colleagues, and adopted martyred expressions. She promptly made us more tea and brought in large slices of homemade cake.

After a little discussion with her husband she said, "I know what we will do. There are a couple of sofas in our sitting room. I will get blankets and you can sleep there. You don't want to stay on that old hilltop.

Nobody is going up there. And from what I've seen there's nothing to steal anyway."

These were our sentiments exactly. We thanked her profusely and said we would just make a quick inspection to see if all was quiet and then take up their kind offer. "Suppose it rains, have they given you umbrellas?" We had to explain to her the RAF did not issue umbrellas to their Guards, but we would be all right. She left the door unlocked so we could come and go as we pleased.

Out in the darkness with only our inadequate torches to guide us we returned to the crash site. All was silent — except for our curses when we stumbled over brambles and bits of aircraft. We stayed for a while; it seemed completely futile so we returned to the comfort of the cottage. We had another chat to our host and hostess, and were given cocoa and more slices of homemade cake.

After a while we said that we would have a lie down on the sofas and go up to the crash site during the night. We lay down in our clothes. That didn't inconvenience us. The next thing we knew, our host was waking us up and telling us it was nearly seven o'clock, and his wife was making the breakfast. And a splendid cooked breakfast it was. After thanking them for their kindness and hospitality we made our way back to the crash site.

Before long the same Sergeant and his working party arrived in a lorry. "Expect you had a rough night."

"Not too bad," we replied stoically.

The lorry took us back to camp, we reported to the Armament Officer and were given the rest of the day off.

As the weeks went by it seemed clear from the newspapers that the war in Europe would soon be over, and sure enough on May 7th Germany surrendered. The following day was declared a Public Holiday and except for those on essential duties we were given the day off. Jack and I decided to go to Doncaster to join in any celebrations that might be taking place. When we arrived it seemed that the celebrations consisted of heavy drinking in the pubs by the many servicemen who had come to town. My one enduring memory of that day is of half a dozen Airmen solemnly walking in single file up the middle of the main street, each one with a pint pot of beer on his head. They must have been relatively sober to manage this balancing act.

The visit to Doncaster was the extent of our jolifications. I had been on leave to Frome earlier in the year; there would be no chance of celebrating at home for some time.

Now that the war in Europe was over we naturally wondered what would happen next. The war in the Far East looked as if it might continue for some time and it seemed possible, or even probable, that some of us might be sent out there. The Government had already published its demobilisation plans. "Demob Numbers" were to be allocated to each serviceman, based on age and length of service: those with the smallest numbers going home first.

My number was 37, and the prediction was that I might have to serve another eighteen months to two years. Jack's number was in the early twenties; he would be demobbed much earlier. There was much discussion in the Armoury. The older men cheerfully forecast that youngsters with numbers above 35 would certainly be sent to the Far East.

One middle-aged joker even suggested that young Armourers might be dropped behind Japanese lines, so that their knowledge of explosives could be put to good use in assisting in acts of sabotage. He was promptly upended and rolled on the floor by several "Young Armourers" to make it clear that this kind of prophesy was not welcome.

Earlier in the year, a notice announced that when hostilities in Europe ceased an Educational Vocational and Training scheme would be introduced in all RAF stations to assist Airmen in their return to civilian life. The Government would introduce an examination solely for ex-servicemen, equivalent of the old school certificate — a bit like the present-day GCSEs — and would be accepted as such by all employers. The new training scheme would enable servicemen to study for this exam during working hours and Instructors would be provided, not only for this, but also for other courses.

Any Airman who had been educated to at least School Certificate standard could apply for training as an Instructor. If selected to fill an Instructor Post he would be given the rank of Acting Sergeant. On reading the last sentence I applied straight away. I found to my surprise that I was the only Armourer with the necessary qualifications for training as an Instructor.

I disregarded the gloomy warnings of some of the others that it was just a trick to ensnare ex-Grammar School boys, and that as soon as we were on the course we would be taught Japanese and shipped out to the Far East. The weeks went by and I heard nothing further about the course so I forgot about it.

A few weeks after VE Day there was a blow to our morale when Station Orders listed a number of Airmen to be transferred to the Army. We realised that now the war in Europe was over there would be much less work at RAF Stations, but we didn't expect the reduction in numbers to start so quickly. There were several Armourers on the list and one of them was Peter who had been with us since our North Battleford days.

We were particularly concerned about Peter going into the Army, because he just couldn't march. He seemed quite incapable of swinging his arms in the normal way, they either moved the same way as his legs, or were held stiffly at his side. This was not too big a disadvantage in the RAF as we did very little parading. We understood that, at his initial training, he was the despair of the Sergeant who kept him out of sight as far as possible.

We feared that the Army would be less tolerant and as someone said in a hushed voice, "Suppose he gets posted to a Guards Regiment!"

We wished him farewell with some trepidation. And as far as Jack and I were concerned it was a break with someone we had been with for more than three years.

We needn't have worried for within two or three weeks he was back with us again. He didn't seem to know exactly why he had been returned. One or two Sergeants had, apparently, been unnecessarily rude about his appearance and the way he marched; and an Officer had then said it might be better if he returned to his RAF unit.

It was at about this time that an incident occurred that I long remembered. Every day in the middle of the morning a Salvation Army van came round, from which we could buy tea or coffee. I was working with Jack at that time, and it was our practice to buy one big mug of coffee and share it, taking alternative sips.

On this particular morning it was wet; we had retreated into the hangar and sat on a bench with our coffee between us. We had just taken a sip each and remarked how good it was when a pigeon perched directly overhead and emptied its bowel. Plop! Straight into our mug of coffee. "It didn't even touch the sides," Jack observed.

The coffee was beyond redemption; we had no choice but to pour it away. And as the Salvation Army van had gone we couldn't get another drink. The few Airmen who had witnessed the scene were helpless with laughter, which didn't make us any happier. "Perhaps it's an omen," I said. Jack's answer was unprintable.

★ ★ ★

At last I was told that my application to be an EVT Instructor had been approved. I was to go on a three-week course at a small RAF unit near Cambridge. I had chosen history as my preferred subject. When I arrived I found there were a dozen or so of us on the course. Most were Airmen of similar rank to myself, but there were one or two NCOs, and surprisingly an RAF padre who was a Commissioned Officer of the rank of Squadron Leader.

I found the course interesting; it taught us various teaching techniques. For me it was a refreshing change to be on a course that did not deal with guns, bombs or explosives.

We all had to prepare and deliver short presentations on subjects we chose ourselves from the history syllabus: first a ten-minute talk, then one of twenty minutes and finally a half-hour session. Our individual efforts were discussed by the Instructor and the rest of the class. I found this rather daunting, but managed to get through the session somehow.

I remember that my half hour talk was about Chartists and the 1832 Reform Act; the Instructor complimented me on it and said it was delivered with conviction. This pleased me, giving me hope that I might pass the course.

It was easy to get to Cambridge by bus. We used to go there at weekends and marvel at the beauty of the old colleges. I remembered, too, that the flowering trees were particularly lovely at the time we were there. Towards the end of the course we were told that professor George Macauly Trevelyan, the master of Kings College, had heard about our course — training potential history teachers for the RAF — and would be pleased to meet us and show us round his College on Sunday afternoon. This was a great honour as Trevelyan was probably the most eminent British historian of his time, and the author of English Social History, the approved reading for schools for many years.

Most of us were able to go, and we duly turned up at Kings College at the appointed time. The great man arrived dressed very informally in grey flannels and an open-necked shirt and greeted us warmly. He asked us about our course, and then escorted us round the College taking us to parts that were not normally open to tourists, explaining everything in great detail and with remarkable enthusiasm.

At the end of the tour someone commented on a particular painting, and he said he had another by the same artist in his house that he would like to show us. Whereupon he promptly led us all into his house where his wife was entertaining two or three lady friends. With just the briefest explanation to his wife, he escorted us through two or three rooms to the picture and talked about it at length. His wife did not seem unduly disconcerted by the unexpected arrival of a dozen Airmen who trampled through her house in their heavy boots. We thought it could not be the first time she had been surprised by her husband's enthusiasm. Anyway it was a memorable afternoon and we considered it a privilege to meet such an eminent man.

At the end of the course I returned to Sandtoft. After a week or two I was notified that I had passed and would be sent to fill a vacancy for an Instructor when a suitable post arose. I heard no more for several weeks and carried on with my normal work in the Armoury. I had a week's leave, which broke the monotony, and soon after my return was summoned to see the Education Officer who told me that if I wished I could work for him and help with the courses he would be running. He did not have an approved post for an EVT Instructor, so I could not be promoted to Sergeant. This was a disappointment, but I thought I might as well take up the offer and work in the Education Section. I left the armoury and, though I didn't know it at the time, I was never to work as an Armourer again.

CHAPTER
FOURTEEN

The War Was Over

Soon afterwards on August 16th Japan surrendered and the war was over. This took us by surprise, because we all thought the war in the Far East would continue for a long time. We had heard a few weeks previously about the new powerful bomb the Americans had, but we were quite unaware of its devastating effect. There was a public holiday to celebrate victory over Japan: VJ Day. That evening, Jack and I went out for a celebratory drink, and cycled over to Thorne, a village six or seven miles from our camp. We knew a pub there quite well and on this evening it was packed both with RAF and civilians. The celebrations went on right through the night and into the early hours. Eventually at about 5a.m. Jack and I left to cycle back to camp. We were not the last to leave.

Somewhat to our surprise we were quite sober and cycled quietly along deserted country roads back to camp. When we reached our huts I said, "It's all over now, Jack."

"Yes, I wonder how we will get on back in Civvy Street."

My work in the Education section was not particularly demanding. There was one other Airman who, like me, had been on an EVT Instructor's course, and together with the Education Officer we dealt with the few applications received for instruction. I soon discovered that no one wished to study history, but there were a number of applications for refresher courses in Mathematics.

I soon found myself teaching Mathematics, which required me to do some hasty revision to keep ahead of the class. We also ran classes on Current Affairs; attendance at these was compulsory. At one of these Jack and several Armourers were in the front row, which I found daunting. I got through it all right and received the dubious compliment, "You are a better instructor than you were an Armourer."

During this period I was told to report to the Station Warrant Officer; there was a place at Leeds University for an EVT Instructor to do a two-week course on English. It started the following Monday; and I had been selected to go. I pointed out that my specialist subject was History, but he impatiently brushed this objection aside. I was the only EVT Instructor available so I had to go. "You seem to speak English all right, you'll cope."

Like many of the Senior NCOs, he was contemptuous of the EVT scheme, saying they never had it in his young days in the pre-war RAF so why introduce it now the war was over? I had no one else to appeal to; the Education Officer was on leave so I got ready to make my way to Leeds. I was a bit apprehensive about

176

coping with an English course at University level and hoped there wouldn't be an examination at the end.

I saw from my Movement Order that I had been booked into a hotel in Leeds. This impressed me, as Airmen were not normally provided with such accommodation. I was even more impressed to be given quite a large room at the front of the hotel; my delight was somewhat diminished when I looked out of the window and saw a railway embankment on the other side of the road. As I watched, a steam train slowly went by making a lot of noise and emitting clouds of steam and smoke. I consoled myself by remembering that I was used to noisy aircraft flying low overhead at night. I was not disturbed too much by the trains; though once or twice I woke with a start thinking a train was coming through the window.

I was not required to be at the University until the civilised time of 10a.m. I discovered, on walking into the centre of the city, that there was a strike of tram drivers. Leeds, like many other cities had trams as well as buses. A number of RAF aircrew had volunteered to be replacement drivers and seemed to be having a great time driving the trams. Strikers sabotaged their efforts from time to time, by using long poles to knock the overhead arm away from the cable carrying power, causing the tram to stop. It was necessary then for the overhead arm to be pushed back in place. It seemed a bit chaotic so, as I had plenty of time, I walked.

I found the university and was taken to a lecture room, which had tiered seats for the students and a rostrum in front for the lecturer. There were about twenty of us of various ranks. I hastily scanned the timetable and was relieved to see there was no mention of an examination at the end. I cannot remember much about the content of the course, except that it dealt mainly with the more modern writers such as James Joyce, Aldous Huxley, and Robert Graves, none of whom had appeared in my local Grammar School curriculum. Anyway I enjoyed it all; it was a pleasant change from life at Sandtoft.

There were two incidents during my stay at Leeds that I remember well.

Three of us decided to go to the theatre to see The Mikado performed by the D'Oyly Carte Company. We had booked seats, but when we arrived we were met by an apologetic manager who said that owing to an error our seats had been double booked. To recompense us he offered us one of the best boxes, which we gladly accepted. I had never been in a box at the theatre before and felt very grand, particularly when we were served coffee and biscuits at the interval.

The other incident also occurred at a theatre, another one in Leeds that I visited to see a play. At the interval I found sitting behind me, with his wife, a former Armourer from Sandtoft who had been discharged as medically unfit some months ago. We had a chat about Sandtoft and they kindly invited me to their home for supper later in the week. I took up their invitation and was made very welcome and had a good evening. He seemed pretty fit so I was left wondering why he had been discharged.

When I returned to Sandtoft it was clear that the camp was being run down. Armourers were being posted away, including Peter who had served with me since North Battleford. This time he was posted to an RAF unit, not to the Army. We said our farewells and never met again.

My friend Bill also left. Because of his age he had a very low demob number and was leaving the RAF to return to "Civvy Street".

I had a week's leave and on my return was told that I was to be posted to RAF Halton, where I would be employed as a clerk. There were still no EVT Instructor vacancies. Halton was a pre-war RAF Training Establishment a few miles from Aylesbury. The other Armourers were similarly to be posted to Halton. One of them was my old friend, Jack. Since leaving Canada we had been posted together to Lindholme, Faldingworth and Sandtoft, and were now going to Halton.

We realised that going to a Training Establishment meant saying goodbye to the free and easy lifestyle at Sandtoft, where there was no perimeter fence or Guard Room, and we could come and go as we pleased so long as we reported for work at the appointed time. I was not sorry to be swapping Nissan Huts for the more comfortable accommodation at a camp built pre-war. Nissan Huts had bare concrete floors and were inadequately heated by the one stove in the centre of the hut. During the winter we generally had to put on extra clothes when we went to bed — such as pullovers and thick socks. We also would not regret leaving behind the smelly latrines and the noisome washing and shower facilities.

On the other hand we had very few parades or inspections and the normal attire for Airmen in winter were Wellington boots, roll neck jumpers and balaclava headgear. Furthermore, we very rarely had a Room Inspection; due to night duties there were always one or two beds occupied by sleeping Airmen during the day. The Orderly Officers kept clear of us when doing their inspection. Consequently, beds remained permanently made up with one blanket laid long ways across the bed and well tucked in so the bed resembled a sleeping bag, and could remain like that for weeks. There were no sheets. Occasionally we dismantled the bedding and shook out the blankets. On these occasions all sorts of oddments were discovered such as odd socks, sundry crumbs and fragments of bread or even a decaying apple core. We imagined that Halton would have more exacting standards.

One reason why Sandtoft is memorable for me is because of the interesting characters I met, some of whom demonstrated a remarkable ability not only to adapt to the circumstances in which they found themselves, but also to prosper. One of these was Harry, an irrepressible cockney with a quick wit and a persuasive manner. Harry had soon made contact with a local bookmaker and became what was known as a "Bookies Runner"; there were no betting shops in those days. Every morning Harry could be seen around the airfield in conversation with other Airmen, and making entries in his notebook. He wore overalls and carried some tools; he was in fact taking bets and collecting the stakes. At lunchtime he cycled into the village to deposit the bets with the bookmaker and return with any winnings. Even in wartime there were some sporting events on which bets could be made. I'm not sure what his official duties were; obviously they did not weigh heavily upon him. Some evenings he could be found serving behind the bar in the village pub, and he was also good at getting hold of items that were rationed. Many an Airman went home on leave with eggs, chicken or cheese thanks to Harry and his many contacts in the village. These activities, no doubt, added considerably to his RAF pay.

Another character was Jim. He was older than most of us and had a wife and family. His RAF trade was Fitter Armourer. What Jim was best at was making cigarette lighters. They were modelled on a popular Ronson of the time; he made them of duralumin from the stocks in the Armoury intended for repairs to gun turrets, etc. and not for the manufacture of lighters. Jim made them so well that the finished article was almost indistinguishable from the commercial model. He added a little extra in the form of the RAF crest. There was a ready sale for these, mostly to Aircrew, for about twenty-five shillings.

Jim was too busy making these to go round selling them. Who better to act as his salesman than Harry with all his contacts? So Harry got a commission of, I think two shillings, for each one sold, and allowing for this sales commission and the cost of components that had to be bought Jim made a clear profit of about £1 per item. He returned to the armoury most evenings to work on his lighters and probably made five or six a week, earning him two or three times as much as his RAF pay. He reckoned he would be well on his way to paying off his mortgage if he could continue to make lighters for a year or two.

Another character that quickly learned how to live comfortably at Sandtoft was Alf. He was in his late thirties, considered middle aged by the rest of us who were mostly in our early twenties. He was a Londoner and probably married, though he never discussed his home life for reasons that soon became apparent.

Alf was an Armourer and mostly worked on a Dispersal Flight at the far end of the airfield. And in common with other Airmen often cycled into the small village that adjoined the perimeter of the airfield to visit the local pub. He there met a lady of about his own age, or perhaps a little older, who lived on her own in a cottage in the village. Whether she was a widow, a spinster or married with a husband away in the services we never discovered, but quite soon Alf moved in with her. He soon created for himself quite a cosy lifestyle, working at the airfield during the day and returning to the cottage in the evening. He ate at the station cookhouse when it suited him.

Soon he became the man of the house, cultivating the little garden and buying a few chickens and making a pen for them. In the evenings he often wore civilian clothes, presumably brought from home and was a habitué of the local pub. He seemed to have been accepted by the village. Once or twice Jack and I cycled over to this pub in the evening and nearly always saw Alf there.

At closing time he would invite us back to the cottage and his lady would serve tea. We were amused to see his slippers had been put to warm in front of the fire, awaiting his return. His idyllic existence continued for some time until the RAF rather inconsiderately posted him away from Sandtoft. I was pretty certain that he would soon adapt to his new surroundings and make himself comfortable. He was a great survivor.

It was Alf and Harry who were the instigators of what we called the "Pig Plot." Alf, through his contacts in the village, discovered that it would be possible to get hold of an "illegal" pig. Meat was rationed and the rearing of pigs and their subsequent slaughter strictly controlled. As with any system there were loopholes, and Harry and Alf were just the people to find and exploit them. There were plenty of Airmen willing to pay for some black market pork to take home on leave. The problem was how to slaughter the pig.

Initially they toyed with the idea of shooting it with a Sten Gun, but thought that the sound of gunfire might attract unwelcome attention. Then Harry discovered that an Airman, named Roy, had been a butcher in civilian life and would be willing to kill and butcher the pig if it was made worth his while. On his next leave, Roy brought his butcher's knives from home and was ready to proceed.

On the appointed day it was arranged that the Armoury van, after it had brought its load of practice bombs and pyrotechnics to the flight hut, would on its

183

return make a short detour to pick up the pig, which was conveniently housed just outside the perimeter of the village. Harry, Alf and Roy went with it, brought the pig back and penned it temporarily in the Flight Hut with the said bombs and pyrotechnics. Harry asked the Flight Mechanics working on a nearby Lancaster to rev up the four engines of the aircraft, so the noise would drown out the squeals of the unfortunate pig. They were quite willing, in return for a few black market cigarettes, which Harry could supply.

All went according to plan. The pig was killed and butchered, and all traces of the operation covered up. A number of Airmen delighted their families by taking home joints of pork. Alf took the offal and, later that week, was joined by Harry and Roy for supper at his cottage, where they no doubt feasted on it and divided up the proceeds from the "Pig Plot".

Another character, though not as astute as Harry and Alf, was Paddy. He was a Flight Mechanic from Southern Ireland, christened Patrick, but always known as Paddy. He never tired of telling us he needn't have been in the RAF, but had volunteered, "To help old England out". He was a cheery individual and well liked, but when conditions were harsh he was frequently teased about volunteering when he could have stayed at home. He took it in good part and said if it hadn't been for all the Irishmen who came over to join the Services the war would have been lost years ago.

When he went on leave he followed an odd routine. He went to the pub the night before and on his return would stagger round the hut saying goodbye to all of us. "I'm not coming back," he would say. "Once I'm in Ireland they can't touch me, it's a neutral country, I volunteered, but they aren't grateful." Then he would recount some telling off he had received from an NCO. We would all wish him goodbye and good luck. He always came back and when asked why would say, "I'll give them one more chance, so I will, but if it doesn't get better I'll be off."

I remember him doing this two or three times while I was at Sandtoft, but he was still there when I left.

The last on my list of well-remembered Sandtoft characters is Ken. Now in all honesty it has to be said that Ken was a thug. He came from a run-down part of Leeds and, as I discovered later, had a rough upbringing. Ken had served two periods in a military prison for striking Senior NCOs and was also a notorious pub brawler, frequently returning at night with a bruised or cut face as a result of fights.

He was not particularly tall, but powerfully built, with broad shoulders, a thick neck and a low forehead with his hairline starting only a few inches above his eyebrows. Also, he was alarmingly strong and could, single handed, lift weights that would take two of us to move. Although he was a fellow Armourer, I tried to keep clear of him as much as I could.

One night we were both on Guard Duty, which meant two hours spent together patrolling the airfield. I had never talked much to him before, but that night we chatted and to my surprise he confided in me about his girlfriend. I can't remember the details; he wished to

185

get in touch with her, but she wasn't on the phone so he didn't know what to do.

Naturally, I suggested sending a letter. He said he hadn't had much of an education and wasn't very good at writing. Impulsively I told him that if he told me what he wanted to say I would put it down on paper for him to copy. He looked surprised, "Would you do that?" and his response made me think he wasn't used to having offers of help. When we returned to the Guard Hut we retreated to a far corner and together composed a letter. The following week he greeted me with a beaming smile; the letter had done the trick and all was well.

Thereafter he treated me as a friend, which I found a bit daunting. On one occasion he told me to let him know if anyone was causing me trouble and he would bash them; I felt that I had been befriended by the equivalent of a semi-trained gorilla.

An example of his direct methods occurred one evening when we were working a bit late putting practice bombs and flares on an aircraft ready for a Night Flying Exercise. There should have been four of us in the team, but one was missing. Consequently it was taking longer than usual.

"Where's Billy?" asked Ken.

"He hasn't turned up," I told him.

"I bet he's sloped off to the Cookhouse to get his supper, I'll get the b . . ." he went on, whereupon he dashed off on his bike. Later, a fellow Armourer in the Cookhouse told me what happened: Ken stormed into the Cookhouse and when he spotted Billy grabbed him by the scruff of the neck and told him that if he didn't return to work immediately he would bash his face in. Billy complied without hesitation.

My final memory of Ken was of one evening in Doncaster when Jack and I were having a quiet drink in a pub we hadn't visited before. There were quite a few Airmen there, but also some Scots Guardsmen. To our dismay Ken came in, and when he spotted us he walked over and joined us, and we had one or two drinks together.

Suddenly Ken said, "Let's have a bit of fun and have a go at these squaddies, it will liven things up a bit."

My blood ran cold, and I quickly said, "Well I'm not feeling too good, Ken. I think it was something I had for tea. I'd better get back to camp." In truth, I did not feel well when I looked at the mountainous size of most of the Guardsmen. With apologies we escaped from the pub, which we afterwards learned was referred to as "The Bucket of Blood" by the locals, because of the frequency of the fights there. Next day we noticed that Ken had some cuts on his face, so presumably he had his "bit of fun".

Towards the end of our stay at Sandtoft, Ken acquired a motorbike on which he would travel to Leeds when he had leave. I don't know how he obtained petrol for it, but I once saw him leaving the MT section carrying a can. We had grave foreboding about Ken on a motorbike knowing his impetuous and belligerent nature. Sure enough, just as we had feared, he had a bad accident and we heard that he was in

Leeds hospital with serious injuries. I often wondered if he survived and if so what happened to him.

RAF Halton

So it was farewell to Sandtoft, as a small group of us made our way to our new station Halton in Buckinghamshire. We went by train from Doncaster to London, and then travelled on the underground via the Bakerloo Line to Amersham, where there was transport to RAF Halton some ten miles away. It was a novelty travelling to an RAF station by underground. Fortunately it was not rush hour or we would not have been very popular with our kit bags and backpacks.

Halton was one of the principal Training Centres for the RAF. It was here that young recruits who entered as boy entrants or apprentices did their initial foot drill, and Trade Training. The centre was well equipped with classrooms and workshops.

We soon realised that if we were to keep out of trouble we would have to smarten ourselves up and abandon the slovenly ways that we had become used to at Sandtoft. It was very much an enclosed camp and we could only enter or leave via the Main Gate; there were checks by the Service Police during normal off duty hours.

Jack and I were in different billets and in due course were given different jobs. It was a typical pre-war built camp with two storey, brick-built barrack blocks that were a bit austere, but warmer and more comfortable than Nissan Huts. We enjoyed the luxury of being able to use the ablutions and toilets within the barrack blocks, and did not have to don our wellies and cross a field as we did at Sandtoft.

We reported for duty next morning and I was assigned for clerical duties at Training Command HQ, which was located in a large country house, a few miles from Halton. This house stood in quite extensive grounds and had formerly belonged to one of the Rothchilds; presumably it had been requisitioned by the RAF at the beginning of the war.

There were about forty or fifty clerical staff and we were transported to and from Halton by lorry.

My job was in the Registry, and the duties were very mundane and did not require much thought. A novelty was that this section was supervised by an elderly civilian Clerical Officer who was regarded as an expert on office procedures, and consequently treated with respect by all uniformed staff, even the Officers. He must have lived nearby as he travelled by bicycle, which he brought into the office to keep it out of the rain. Even this was tolerated, despite it being a bit of a nuisance as staff occasionally fell over it. After I had been in this job for a week or so I was required to take something to the Chief Education Officer, and took the opportunity to tell him that I was a trained EVT Instructor, and was anxious to get a posting. He promised to see what he could do.

Although we were working in different locations I still saw Jack from time to time and we would walk to the nearby village of Wendover and have a drink in one of the many pubs there. Because he was about ten years older than me he had a much lower demob number and expected to be demobbed early in the New Year.

Time passed pretty uneventfully and soon we were approaching the end of the year. Officially, I was on duty on Christmas Day as a Fire Guard, but managed to bribe a young Irishman, who couldn't go home anyway, to take my place. I went home unofficially and greatly enjoyed Christmas with Eileen and the family. It was my first Christmas at home since 1940. On my return, I was able to take leave at the New Year as officially I had been on duty at Christmas, so I saw in the New Year at home. I confidently expected that by next Christmas I would be a civilian; it seemed very likely that my demob number would be reached by the summer of 1946.

CHAPTER
FIFTEEN

1946

Soon after I returned from my New Year leave I had the good news that I was to be posted as an EVT instructor to RAF Locking. This meant that not only would I be promoted to the rank of Sergeant, but I would also be stationed within fairly easy travelling distance of Frome. Locking was a few miles outside Weston-Super-Mare, and there were frequent trains from Weston to Bristol, and a reasonable local train service to Frome.

I sought out Jack to tell him my good news and that evening we had a farewell drink. We had served together at various RAF stations for four and a half years and he had been a very good friend. He, too, was quite excited as he was expecting to be demobbed shortly.

Sadly, after leaving Halton I never saw him again. We corresponded briefly, but this tailed off as Jack was not a great letter writer. Then in 1951 he and his wife had a holiday in the West Country and on their way home stopped off at Frome and called at Flint House. They saw my mother and my brother, but by then Eileen and I were married and living at Banwell, just outside Weston-super-Mare.

Ironically Jack had driven through Weston-super-Mare on his way to Frome and probably passed within a mile or two from where we lived. He spoke to me on the phone from Flint House, but that was all. I never heard from him again.

On leaving Halton I was given a weekend leave and was able to go home before reporting to Locking. Whilst I was at home Eileen sewed on my new stripes so I was able to set off to my new station properly attired as a Sergeant.

RAF Locking

On arriving I was signed in and shown to my new quarters. I found I would be sharing a room with another EVT Instructor who was also a fairly new Sergeant. His name was Sid, and our meeting at Locking was the start of a long-term friendship that continued long after we had both left the RAF.

Sid had been at Locking a few weeks and was able to show me round and explain the regulations appertaining to the Sergeants' Mess of which I was now a member. The food was much the same as in the Airmen's Mess, but better prepared and presented, and the Mess fees we all paid provided a few little extras. There were cloths on the tables and cutlery was provided; I no longer had to carry a knife, fork, spoon and mug with me, as I did as an Airman.

Adjoining the dining room was a large lounge comfortably furnished with armchairs, and the day's newspapers were available. The senior member of the Mess was the Station Warrant Officer who was treated with respect. And his favourite chairs, both in the dining room and the lounge, were pointed out to me so that I would not commit the terrible blunder of sitting in them.

The next morning, I was interviewed by the Education Officer and I learned that no one wanted history lessons; I would be teaching Mathematics, English and Civics as there was a demand for all of these subjects. He also advised me to brush up my knowledge of Economics as I might be required to teach that later on. As I knew nothing about Economics, brushing up in my case meant getting a book from the Station Library, starting on page one and working my way through the book.

I found there was only one other Sergeant EVT Instructor in addition to Sid and myself. He was married and lived in Weston-super-Mare travelling to and from his home by bike each day. We were kept fairly busy with our classes; the Education Officer helped out occasionally.

A little later on a newly commissioned WAAF officer arrived to swell our numbers. She seemed a little out of her depth in her new role and appeared to be more comfortable in the company of us NCOs than in the Officers' Mess.

All Sergeants had to take it in turns to be Orderly Sergeant for the day and it wasn't long before I had my first experience of this duty. The first task was to go into each of the Airmen's billets at 6.30a.m. shouting "Wakey, wakey!" at the top of one's voice, and adding to the din by picking up the poker or coal shovel and hammering on the coal bucket, whilst ignoring the muttered curses from the Airmen.

After this, it was necessary to shout "Any sick?" in an equally loud voice, and making a note of the name and number of anyone responding. The RAF wanted any ailments to be declared at 6.30a.m. Then the patients would parade outside the Guardroom at 8.30a.m. ready to be marched to the sick quarters by the Orderly Sergeant who would already have a list of their names. It was much tidier this way and ignored the fact that someone woken from sleep in such an abrupt manner might need more than the few seconds allowed to decide whether they were sufficiently ill to need medical attention. It was not impossible to report sick at times other than 6.30 in the morning, but it was not encouraged.

My next duty after reveille was to go to the Airmen's Mess at 8a.m. to see if there were any complaints about the breakfast. Both Orderly Officers and Orderly Sergeants were supposed to go, but I found the Orderly Officer sometimes missed the breakfast duty, presumably because he was too busy, perhaps because he was having his own breakfast.

On my first time as Orderly Sergeant it was fish for breakfast and I was aware of this long before I reached the Airmen's Mess. It smelled pretty foul, but strangely I got no response when I walked round the dining room shouting, "Any complaints?" Some Airmen were gazing sadly on what was on their plates, apparently too dispirited to complain. On the other hand a few sturdy individuals were eating the smelly breakfast with apparent relish. I made good my escape and thought I had got off lightly.

After this I had to go to the Guardroom, to march those who had reported sick to the Sick Quarters. Inevitably there were more people on the parade than had reported at 6.30 a.m. Apparently at this point the Orderly Sergeant should sigh heavily in protest at this additional burden and add the names to the list. The reason given for not reporting at the appointed time was invariably that they were in the lavatory. Occasionally there was a variation such as their throat was so bad that on waking they couldn't speak. After I had handed the men and the list to the Hospital Orderly I was able to resume my normal duties until lunchtime.

The Orderly Officer put in an appearance at lunchtime and together we walked round the Airmen's Mess whilst I shouted "Any complaints?" There weren't any, but rather than making good our escape the Orderly Officer insisted on inspecting the kitchen. The NCO in charge was summoned, and turned out to be a large and formidable looking WAAF Sergeant who did little to conceal her annoyance at being interrupted at a busy time.

Quite undeterred the young Orderly Officer poked around the kitchen, opening cupboards and peering into food containers, whilst I was conscious of the WAAF Sergeant's mounting fury. I wondered how long it would be before she exploded and reached for a meat cleaver. Mercifully the Officer finished his inspection before that point was reached. Afterwards he told me that he believed in keeping the kitchen staff up to scratch. Fortunately the inspection of the evening meal went without incident.

My final duty at 6p.m. was to check that everyone detailed for Guard Duty that night had turned up. If not the Orderly Sergeant was empowered to make up the number by detailing any Airmen, picked at random. This was normally done by going into the nearest billet and selecting the first Airman seen. But this practice was well known, and the sight of the Orderly Sergeant approaching the billet at that time of day was a signal for a rapid exit out of the back door. Fortunately, on this occasion the full compliment of Airmen was present and I didn't have to press gang anyone to fill vacancies. After this I was merely required to spend the rest of the evening in the Sergeants' Mess, "on call" if required. I was not at Locking long enough for the Orderly Sergeant's job to come round very often and fortunately nothing untoward ever happened.

Life at Locking was quite pleasant and I quite enjoyed my instructional duties. Furthermore I was able to go home most weekends, which was a bonus. The EVT Sergeant who was married and lived in Weston-Super-Mare was a music lover. Occasionally he would invite Sid and I to his home to spend an evening listening to some of his records. He had a large collection and would play selected items for us.

One evening he invited our young WAAF Officer who was very much on her own, as there were very few of them at Locking. She accepted enthusiastically and we had a very pleasant evening. The weather was good and, as it was comfortable walking distance, the three of us decided to walk back.

To pass the time I recounted some of the funny things that had happened whilst I was in Canada. This really amused her to such an extent that, at one point, she was almost helpless with laughter and we had to stop for her to recover. I was surprised, and a little flattered that she was so responsive. Sid said afterwards that she laughed so much that he feared she would wet herself.

Sid was a pleasant companion and we got on well together. He was older than I, married and had a young son. He lived in Swindon and was also able to get home at weekends. We travelled by train to Bristol, where we would go our separate ways. We both reminisced about pre-war days and I was quite impressed when he told me that on winter afternoons he would go to the shops and buy ice cream to go with their tinned fruit. In Frome, there was nowhere at that time of year where you could buy ice cream, it was solely a summer delicacy.

Sid and I shared a room and occasionally Station Orders would announce that there was to be a Room Inspection by the Adjutant. On these occasions our abode had to be smartened up, tops of cupboards dusted and the floor polished. Once, Sid had done some dusting and was on his hands and knees polishing the floor whilst I was lying on the bed reading, and pointing out the bits he had missed.

Suddenly Sid stopped working and looked at me, "I'm older than you. I'm senior to you. And I'm bigger than you. So why am I polishing the floor and you are lying on the bed watching me?" I really had no reply to that except to promise to do it next time.

However, there was not to be a next time as I received the long awaited notification that my demobilisation would be soon and I was to return to RAF Halton to await it. Sid, though older than I, had less service so he had a little longer to wait. When we said goodbye we thought it unlikely that we would meet again. Happily it was not to be so.

We kept in touch by the occasional letter and then when Eileen and I were living in Bath in 1949/50 Sid and his family moved there and we were able to visit. When we left Bath and for many years after, we continued to correspond and sometimes when Eileen and I were on holiday we used to visit. We corresponded on a regular basis until the 1980s when ill health prevented Sid from continuing.

★ ★ ★

When I left Locking I thought I was unlikely to see it again, but five years later Eileen and I lived for a while at Banwell only a mile or so from Locking Camp.

Halton (again)

I had a weekend at home before going to Halton. Travelling to Frome station on the Sunday evening to catch the train to London, I saw on the platform two former school friends, Ed and Fred, who were also going there. They were both in the RAF; Ed was a Leading Aircraftsman (LAC) and Fred a Flying Officer. Ed was a clerk and Fred Aircrew. He had survived a tour of operations as a navigator in Stirling aircraft and had been commissioned at the end. We had not all met up since the start of the war, as our leaves hadn't coincided. We, therefore, had plenty to talk about on our journey to Paddington, there we separated and went our various ways.

At Halton I was told to report to Training Command Headquarters, where I had worked as a clerk before going to Locking. The following morning I was on the RAF coach to the Headquarters building, to report to the Adjutant. Outside his office were another half dozen Sergeants all, like me, waiting to be demobbed. Eventually we all went in, but did not find him very welcoming. He didn't endear himself to us by saying that if we thought we were going to idle away the time before our demob date — which we did — we were going to be disappointed — which we were. He went on to say there were another ten days before we would go to the demob centre, and he intended to find us some useful employment during that time.

This was bad news, and it got worse. He needed two NCOs to supervise a group of German Prisoners Of War who were employed on odd jobs around the HQ building. Supervision was necessary, because a day or two ago one of the prisoners had written "SWINEHUND" (pig dog) on the Air Vice Marshal's window. I thought this very funny (I still do) and laughed merrily, but stopped suddenly when I realised I was the only one laughing and the Adjutant was glaring at me.

"It's not funny," he shouted. "It was a gross insult to the most senior officer at this HQ." I tried to compose myself and look suitably outraged, but the damage had been done. The Adjutant immediately appointed me Supervisor, assisted by another Sergeant who perhaps smiled at the wrong time.

Off we went to meet the POWs; we were both a bit worried about our new responsibility. As my colleague said, "If one of them escapes there will be a Court of Enquiry, and this would delay our demob."

We found there were about twenty; all ex-Africa Corps and a tough looking bunch. The senior man was a Sergeant Major who was an imposing individual, well over six feet tall and with features that looked as if they had been carved out of granite. Mercifully, he could speak some English and was quite affable. Later he told me that he was quite impressed by the smartness of the RAF and the high standard of their marching. He had only seen Halton, where Airmen were being specially drilled for a Victory Parade march, and I thought if only he could see the scruffiness of the Airmen at RAF Airfields.

The POWs were mostly engaged on gardening duties in the grounds, and some cleaning. The Sergeant Major would strut around and generally supervise. Every time he saw a car coming up the drive with an Officer in it he would call his men to attention and give an impressive salute. If we were in the vicinity we felt we had to do the same, but our salutes were not up to his standard. Twice a day the tea wagon came round providing hot drinks, and we felt we had to buy a drink for any POWs in the area, and they nearly all were. As my fellow Sergeant said, "This job is going to cost us a fortune." And we wondered if there was anything in the Geneva Convention about free drinks for prisoners.

The days up to our demob date seemed to drag and my colleagues were forever walking round counting the POWs and saying things like, "Have you seen that ginger haired one lately?" We also thought it important not to let them be unsupervised when near the Air Vice Marshal's window. Mercifully, none went missing, perhaps the free drinks helped, nor were there any fresh insults.

And at long last it was time for me to report to the Demob Centre at RAF Cardington in Bedfordshire. The date of my demobilisation, for which I had waited so long, was 12th June 1946.

CHAPTER
SIXTEEN

RAF Cardington

When I arrived at Cardington I discovered that the Demobilisation Centre was in a huge hangar. In the 1930s airships were built here, including the R100, and the ill-fated R101. The latter had crashed in France on its maiden flight with great loss of life amongst the crew and its passengers, including the Secretary of State for Air and several other dignitaries. This calamity virtually put a stop to the building of large airships in this country. Since then the hangars had been used by the RAF for various purposes, and had now become its demobilisation centre.

There was much paperwork to complete, during which I had the good news that I had served just sufficient time as a Sergeant, 180 days, to qualify for a gratuity based on Sergeant's pay. I was also told that I would have two months' leave with pay after I had been demobbed. Rather less welcome information was that I would be classed as a "Reservist" and should hostilities commence again I would be recalled. For this reason I was allowed to retain my uniform and was provided with a form that would entitle me to draw the sum of five shillings at any post office should remobilisation be ordered. I was not too worried by these warnings as I thought remobilisation would never happen, and it never did during my time.

I was then allowed into the clothing store to select my civilian clothing, which consisted of hat, raincoat, suit, shoes, socks, shirts, tie and underwear. There was a vast array of these items in various shades and sizes, and Airmen in various stages of undress trying them on. For my suit I selected what I thought was a nice worsted, dark blue with a herring bone pattern. I was quite pleased with it; though a little less pleased a few weeks later when one of my aunts said it was like the suit they issued to inmates of the workhouse. I was later, in 1947, to get married in it.

Apart from my school cap I had never possessed a civilian hat; I chose what I thought was a rather nice trilby. This was destined to have a very short life: a week or two after my demob I was wearing it whilst walking Eileen home on a dark and stormy night; it blew off over a fence into a muddy building site. I never saw it again.

The other items were selected without trouble until I came to the underwear. The store man apologised and said he only had underpants in the very large size. We were allowed two pairs each and when he produced them it was clear that very large was an understatement. They were enormous and I couldn't imagine any man they would fit, they seemed more suitable for a medium sized elephant. It was that or nothing as clothing was still rationed, and I thought they might come in handy for something. Indeed they did, because later on Eileen cut them up and made knickers out of the material.

When I had made my selection I took the various items to a counter at the end of the hangar and the store man packed them in a large cardboard box. These distinctive cardboard boxes became quite a common sight and you knew that the servicemen carrying them were on their way home from a demob centre. We were allowed to retain one of each uniform item and my battledress was eventually handed over to my brother who wore it around the farm, and the boots were useful for gardening.

I visited Cardington once more some thirty years later when working for the MOD. It was still being used by the RAF. On that occasion I met one of the very few survivors from the R101 disaster.

So wearing my uniform for the last time, and carrying my new civilian clothes in a cardboard box, I made my way home to Frome. After nearly five and a half years my service in the RAF was over, and I had to face up to the problems I would encounter on returning to civilian life, and finding suitable employment.

And Then . . .

After leaving the RAF Eric returned to his pre-war job as a clerk on the Longleat Estate. He and Eileen were married in February 1947 and two daughters were born in the 1950s. Shortly after his marriage he joined the Civil Service. Eric's work took the family from Frome to live in Bath, Banwell (Somerset), Bunny (Notts), Sutton Coldfield and finally to Ashtead in Surrey. By the time he retired in 1981 he had risen to the grade of Principal in the Ministry of Defence.

Surrey had become "home" — though he never lost his great affection for Somerset, and visited regularly to see family and friends.

Eric and Eileen enjoyed a long and happy retirement in Ashtead where they became well known and loved members of the community, and where Eileen still lives.

Jean Gardner and Katherine Moon 2005